THE SACRED PROJECT OF AMERICAN SOCIOLOGY

THE SACRED PROJECT
OF AMERICAN SOCIOLOGY

Christian Smith

OXFORD
UNIVERSITY PRESS

OXFORD
UNIVERSITY PRESS

Oxford University Press is a department of the University of Oxford.
It furthers the University's objective of excellence in research, scholarship,
and education by publishing worldwide.

Oxford   New York
Auckland   Cape Town   Dar es Salaam   Hong Kong   Karachi
Kuala Lumpur   Madrid   Melbourne   Mexico City   Nairobi
New Delhi   Shanghai   Taipei   Toronto

With offices in
Argentina   Austria   Brazil   Chile   Czech Republic   France   Greece
Guatemala   Hungary   Italy   Japan   Poland   Portugal   Singapore
South Korea   Switzerland   Thailand   Turkey   Ukraine   Vietnam

Oxford is a registered trade mark of Oxford University Press
in the UK and certain other countries.

Published in the United States of America by
Oxford University Press
198 Madison Avenue, New York, NY 10016

Library of Congress Cataloging-in-Publication Data
Smith, Christian, 1960–
The sacred project of American sociology / Christian Smith.
p.   cm. — (Philosophische analyse = Philosophical analysis)
Includes bibliographical references and index.
ISBN 978–0–19–937713–8 (hardcover : alk. paper) —
ISBN 978–0–19–937714–5 (ebook) — ISBN 978–0–19–937716–9 (online content)
1. Religion and sociology—United States. 2. United States—Religion. I. Title.
BL60.S565 2014
306.60973—dc23
                                                2013050538

1   3   5   7   9   8   6   4   2

Printed in the United States of America on acid-free paper

*For sociologists more committed
to the best possible understandings and explanations of
the truth about social life—whatever they may be—
than to making social life conform to their
predetermined ideological commitments.*

"We despise all reverences and all the objects of reverence which are outside the pale of our own list of sacred things. And yet, with strange inconsistency, we are shocked when other people despise and defile the things which are holy to us."

Mark Twain, *Following the Equator*

CONTENTS

INTRODUCTION

Sociology as an academic discipline appears on the surface to be a secular, scientific enterprise. Its founding fathers were mostly atheists. Its basic operating premises are secular and naturalistic. And its disciplinary culture is indifferent and sometimes hostile to religion, often for what are thought of as rationalistic and scientific reasons. American sociology's early historical professionalization also involved the intentional marginalization of Christian Social-Gospel activists who wanted to claim a place in the newly forming scientific discipline.[1] Sociologists today are disproportionately not religious, compared to all Americans, and often irreligious people.[2] And a great deal of sociology is devoted to showing that the ordinary world of everyday life as it *seems* to most people is not *really*

1. Christian Smith, 2003, *The Secular Revolution: Power, Interest, and Conflict in the Secularization of American Public Life*, Berkeley: University of Califorina Press, pp. 97–159.
2. Elaine Howard Ecklund and Christopher Scheitle, 2007, "Religion among Academic Scientists: Distinctions, Disciplines, and Demographics," *Social Problems*, 54(2): 289–307; Martin Trow and Associates, 1969, *Carnegie Commission National Survey of Higher Education: Faculty Study*, Berkeley: University of California at Berkeley, Survey Research Center; Martin Trow and Associates, 1984, *Carnegie Commission National Survey of Higher Education: Faculty Study*, Berkeley: University of California at Berkeley, Survey Research Center.

what is going on—in short, to debunking appearances.[3] Thus, for example, ordinary people's naïve experiences of religious faith and sacred practice ought not to be taken seriously on their own terms, but are better understood through the sociological reinterpretations of their scientific meanings and causes, in terms of concepts like resource exchanges, status struggles, coping mechanisms, gender inequalities, class interests, social control, etc.

My purpose here is to show that, to the contrary, the secular enterprise that everyday sociology *appears* to be pursuing is actually not what is *really* going on at sociology's deepest level. Contemporary American sociology is, rightly understood, actually a profoundly *sacred* project at heart. Sociology today is in fact animated by *sacred* impulses, driven by *sacred* commitments, and serves a *sacred* project. We might even say that American sociology's project is "spiritual," as long as we understand the full breadth and depth of what "spiritual" in this case means. By conducting this self-reflexive, tables-turning, cultural and institutional sociology of the profession of American sociology itself, I show in what follows that this allegedly secular discipline ironically expresses Emile Durkheim's inescapable sacred, exemplifies its own versions of Marxist false consciousness, and generates a spirited reaction against Max Weber's melancholically observed disenchantment of the world.[4]

---

3. Peter Berger, 1963, *Invitation to Sociology*, New York: Anchor, p. 38.
4. In one way, then, this book can be read as "a sociology-of-religion of sociology-the-discipline," since this book studies a sacred movement, although in this case a secular sacred movement. Secularity and secularism are areas in which sociologists of religion have increasingly focused in recent years, "the secular" becoming more properly understood as not a neutral, default human position or category, but instead a contingently situated, particular stance and type, the exigencies of which are worth empirical investigation. See, for example, Craig Calhoun, Mark Jurgensmeyer, and Jonathan VanAntwerpen, 2011, *Rethinking Secularism*, New York: Oxford University Press; Phil Zuckerman, 2009, *Atheism and Secularity*, New York: Praeger; Talal Asad, 2003, *Formations of the Secular*, Palo Alto: Stanford University Press; Courtney Bend and Ann Taves, 2012, *What Matters?: Ethnographies of Value in a Not So Secular Age*, New York: Columbia University Press.

American sociology, in short, does not escape the analytic net that it casts over the rest of the ordinary world. Sociology itself is a part of that very human, very social, often very sacred and spiritual world. I write, therefore, to help American sociology break the magical spells that it has cast on itself using incantations conjuring the misrecognition of its own deepest impulses, in order to prompt an honest reckoning with the profoundly sacred nature of its project.

Chapter 1

The Argument

I begin my case by defining the basic terms of my argument, then stating the argument itself, and finally exploring some important qualifications and implications.

DEFINING TERMS

My argument does not turn on a tricky play on words. I mean exactly what my terms ordinarily suggest. By "sacred," I mean *things set apart from the profane and forbidden to be violated*, exactly what the sociologist Emile Durkheim meant by the term.[1] Sacred matters are never ordinary, mundane, or instrumental. They are reverenced, venerated, and defended as sacrosanct by the social groups that hold them as sacred. Sacred things are set apart from all that is common and profane, as if they were holy. Sacred objects are hallowed, revered, and honored as beyond questioning or disrespect. They can never be defiled, defied, or desecrated by any infringement or

1. Durkheim, 1995 [1912], *The Elementary Forms of Religious Life*, New York: Free Press.

denigration. Things sacred thus have particular powers to motivate and direct human action on their behalf and for their protection. This is exactly the character of the dominant project of American sociology.

I have also said that sociology's project might be considered spiritual, when that term is properly understood, and so I will also use that word in what follows in addition to "sacred." By "spiritual," I mean that dimension of human life that concerns the most profound, meaningful, and transcendent visions of human existence, feeling, and desires. Spiritual matters as I mean that here concern beliefs, longings, and experiences—both conscious and unconscious—about the greatest and highest good, truth, rightness, value, vitality, meaning, and beauty. Such irrepressible concerns of the "human spirit" speak and respond to what is most worth living for, what purposes merit our devotion, what goods are to be most prized, what ends are worth dedicating ourselves to realize. These concerns and commitments are about life dedication, submission, and steadfastness. Spiritual matters contrast with the more mundane, material, and instrumental affairs of life. Human spiritual questions transcend interests of mere survival or subsistence or routine. They focus the mind, will, and emotions on higher visions, deeper meanings, and more profound aspirations in life. Things "spiritual" of this nature have a quality that transcends instrumental, means–ends rationality. They sustain and guide people with visions drawn from the deepest wellsprings of their lives, what some call the depths of the human "heart," in ways that actually pre-rationally and a-rationally govern, rather than are governed by, preferences, rationality, and calculated choices.

This is the sense in which I say that American sociology is driven and governed by not only a sacred but also a spiritual project. To be clear, my use of "spiritual" is here decidedly *anthropocentric*, resting its meaning not on belief in the metaphysical existence of ghosts, but instead on the experience and motivating force of "the human spirit." In this usage, "spiritual" need not be concerned with the supernatural, God, gods, spooks, etcetera, or necessarily have anything directly to do with religion. This is just as the contemporary phrase, "I am spiritual but not religious," suggests. Things spiritual may and often do connect to religion, but they do not have to.[2] People and movements can be devoted to "spiritual" (and sacred) causes that are not substantively religious.[3] One can be both spiritual in this sense and secular. Many sociologists in fact are exactly that, as I aim to show below, as is the discipline of American sociology collectively. At the same time, a sociological view compels us to see that certain factors—sociology's place in western and American history, and the common American historical and contemporary interaction of human spiritual concerns (as I define that above) with religious traditions—mean that sociology's spiritual project is indeed in some ways structurally and culturally related to religion, even if it itself is not directly religious in any usual sense of that concept.

What about my other terms? By "project" I mean a complex, purposive endeavor requiring concerted effort sustained over time to mobilize, coordinate, and deploy resources of different kinds to achieve a desired but challenging goal. Projects can range from

2. See, for example, Nancy T. Ammerman, 2013, "Spiritual But Not Religious?: Beyond Binary Choices in the Study of Religion," *Journal for the Scientific Study of Religion*, 52: 258–278.
3. In this sense, I mean "spiritual" similarly to how Jerry Muller describes Georg Lukác and Hans Freyer as "spiritual guides" on the left (of the Communist Party) and the right (the state, following Hegel), respectively, in mid-twentieth century Europe—both intellectuals were secular, yet wrote about "transnational, transethnic, universal community," the "yearning for an intense emotional commitment to a community of purpose," and "the experience of subordination to a higher, collective purpose," the realization of which intellectuals were to play the crucial role in promoting—and in that sense they were spiritual visionaries and leaders. Muller, 2002, *The Mind and the Market: Capitalism in Western Thought*, New York: Anchor Books, pp. 274–278.

building a deck off one's house's back step to fomenting a politi-cal revolution to establish a social utopia. American sociology is engaged in "a project," I am saying, one that is deeply sacred in nature.

By "sociology," I mean the professionalized academic discipline located in the social sciences of most colleges and universities in American higher education, organized in the form of departments that offer academic degrees for undergraduate majors and some-times through master's and doctoral programs, whose faculty are expected to teach, research, and publish scholarship. My story may apply to sociology as conducted outside of the United States too—I do not know enough to say for sure. But I do know American sociol-ogy quite well enough to make my case here, and so will focus on it.[4] What I describe here about sociology is obviously also embedded in the intellectual and moral culture of American higher education and elite, knowledge-class culture more broadly, though I spend little time here exploring that larger context. Also, importantly, by speaking of "sociology" as a whole, I am not claiming that each and every American sociologist is committed to the spiritual project I describe below. Many are, but some are not. Yet *some* individual so-ciologists do not matter here, since, as sociologists well know, *the collective power of dominant institutionalized sociocultural systems* is much more important than this or that individual commitment and possible dissent in particular cases. Many American sociologists are definitely and actively committed to sociology's sacred proj-ect, some are more passively so, and some are not at all. In the end,

---

4. Other disciplines in the academy also have their own projects, many of which may also be sacred, but addressing them is beyond my purpose here. But see, for example, Robert Nelson, 2002, *Economics as Religion: From Samuelson to Chicago and Beyond*, State Col-lege, PA: Pennsylvania State University Press; Robert Nelson, 2009, *The New Holy Wars: Economic Religion Versus Environmental Religion in Contemporary America*, State College, PA: Pennsylvania State University Press; Paul Vitz, 1995, *Psychology as Religion: The Cult of Self-Worship*, Grand Rapids: Eerdmans.

that all still adds up to American sociology as a *collective* enterprise being and having a sacred project.[5]

Crucial to my argument is this fact: the *sacred* and *spiritual* nature of American sociology's project is not commonly, if ever, acknowledged for what it is. Sociology misrecognizes its very own project. How instead does sociology typically think of itself? What self-images might American sociology actually recognize? Some sociologists think of the discipline as the "science of society." Sociology studies human social life using "the scientific method," just like other sciences study particular aspects of the natural world and universe. Other sociologists who are less comfortable with the idea of sociology being "scientific" think of the discipline more generally as "the study of social groups, institutions, and structures." These are the kinds of self-descriptions found in most sociology survey textbooks. Officially, the American Sociological Association (ASA) offers a characteristically inclusive[6] approach, taking multiple stabs of self-understanding in its definition of the discipline:

> Sociology is: the study of society; a social science involving the study of the social lives of people, groups, and societies; the study of our behavior as social beings, covering everything from the analysis of short contacts between anonymous individuals on the street to the study of global social processes; the scientific study of social aggregations, the entities through

5. I write that sociology both *is* and *has* a sacred project. Both are true. Insofar as enough American sociologists collectively possess (have) and pursue this sacred project with such devotion, American sociology has actually *become* that sacred project, such that it is now impossible to think about the very nature and purpose of American sociology apart from its defining sacred and spiritual project—that endeavor has come to constitute what American sociology itself at heart *is*.

6. Inclusion—not leaving anyone out, and so possibly feeling bad—itself being a central value in sociology's spiritual project, even if, in the end, in the case of ASA's self-definition, it comes at the cost of conceptual cogency.

THE SACRED PROJECT OF AMERICAN SOCIOLOGY

which humans move throughout their lives; an overarching unification of all studies of humankind, including history, psychology, and economics.[7]

Sociology, by this account, is a "study" (mentioned twice) and a "science" (ditto) focused for its subject matter on society; the lives of people, groups, and societies; human behavior; social aggregations; and all of humankind—this discipline is also said to provide the all-encompassing synthetic integration of all other disciplines concerning humans and their knowledge about humanity.[8] Some of this may be right. But note that none of it admits to advancing a sacred project. In fact, it all sounds quite general, abstract, and neutral—almost antiseptic. That is in part because this definition of what sociology *is* focuses exclusively, if vaguely, on what sociology *does*, not, more tellingly, on the *purposes* or *ends* for *doing what it does*. We find no "in order to" clauses in this definition. According to the ASA, then, American sociology is an activity of scientific study, with no particular (stated) purpose or goal in view—at least not one that defines the discipline or can be publicly stated.

I propose, by contrast, that American sociology definitely does have an "in order to" project, one that is *sacred*.[9] But, if so, then why do not ASA or sociology survey textbooks say so? Two reasons. First, sociology's spiritual project is so ubiquitous and taken for granted in the discipline that it has become invisible to most sociologists themselves. So deeply is this sacred project lodged in the soul of

7. http://www.asanet.org/about/sociology.cfm (accessed September 24, 2013).
8. Just don't try to tell that last bit to economists, psychologists, and historians—or anthropologists or political scientists.
9. I intentionally use the language of sociology as a collective actor in this paper (e.g., "sociology is committed . . .") as a writing convenience. I recognize that human persons are the real actors, ultimately. My following of this convention, however, always involves the qualification noted above, that not all individual sociologists are committed to the discipline's spiritual project. Readers who are not hard-core methodological individualists should have no problem with this style of discourse.

American sociology, and so obvious is its appeal, that ordinary sociologists find it impossible to make it the independent object of explicit observation and analysis. It is central to sociology's orthodoxy
and habitus, and so goes unnoticed. Second, publicly naming and
overtly embracing this sacred and spiritual project would threaten
the scientific authority and scholarly legitimacy of academic sociology on which the project itself depends for success. Keeping the
sacred project misrecognized, implicit, and unexamined provides
an escape hatch of "plausible deniability" that is politically necessary. This of course requires that sociologists carefully exempt their
own discipline from their otherwise searching sociological gaze.
But, since sociologists are all too humans, that is entirely doable.

THE PROJECT

What actually *is* the sacred project of American sociology, then? We
might *start* by saying that sociology is about something like *exposing, protesting, and ending through social movements, state regulations,
and government programs all human inequality, oppression, exploitation, suffering, injustice, poverty, discrimination, exclusion, hierarchy,
constraint and domination by, of, and over other humans (and perhaps
animals and the environment)*. This would be accurate. But this formulation does not go deep enough to uncover the more basic and
determining assumptions about philosophical anthropology and
normative goods that sociology's sacred project presupposes. If we
want to really understand sociology well, we need to dig harder.
Sociology's deeper sacred project is more fully and accurately described as follows. American sociology as a collective enterprise is
at heart committed to the visionary project of *realizing the emancipation, equality, and moral affirmation of all human beings as autonomous, self-directing, individual agents (who should be) out to live*

7

their lives as they personally so desire, by constructing their own favored identities, entering and exiting relationships as they choose, and equally enjoying the gratification of experiential, material, and bodily pleasures. That is the deeper vision that undergirds and justifies the first description about ending oppression, etcetera. It provides the more positive, constructive account for why all of those bad things need to be exposed, protested, and ended. Without this Durkheimian sacred project powerfully animating the soul of American sociology, the discipline would be a far smaller, drabber, less significant endeavor—perhaps it would not even have survived as an academic venture to this day.

American sociology's sacred project does not embody one single ideology or program. It is rather an unstable amalgam of variously accumulated historical and contemporary ideas and movements. At its core stands western, *liberal individualism* in the tradition of John Locke, Adam Smith, and John Stuart Mill. That is framed by the larger inheritance of the western (so-called) *Enlightenment*, received in its more skeptical and rationalist modes, in the tradition of Emmanuel Kant ("Dare to think for oneself"[10]), Voltaire (*"La nôtre [religion] est sans contredit la plus ridicule, la plus absurde, et la plus sanguinaire qui ait jamais infecté le monde"*[11]), and Auguste Comte (the founder of positivism, of the discipline of "Sociology" as the "Queen of the Sciences," and of a new, non-theistic "Religion of Humanity" emphasizing altruistic service).[12]

10. Immanuel Kant, *Practical Philosophy*, transl. and ed. Mary J. Gregor, 1996, New York: Cambridge University Press, pp. 15–22.
11. *Letters of Voltaire and Frederick the Great*, 1927, transl. Richard Aldington, New York: Brentano's.
12. Henry May, 1978, The *Enlightenment in America*, New York: Oxford University Press; Gertrude Himmelfarb, 2005, *The Roads to Modernity: The British, French, and American Enlightenments*, New York: Vintage; Smith, 2003, p. 54. One dictionary of sociology also refers to the discipline in similar terms, though without direct reference to Comte: "sociology is sometimes seen (at least by sociologists) as a queen of the social sciences,

But American sociology's sacred project is not simply about bourgeois Enlightenment liberalism. It is also formed by other powerful intellectual, cultural, and political movements. One is the *Marxist tradition*, central to the discipline's theoretical canon, which provides sociology an analytically lambasting, teleologically revolutionary, and socially utopian edge that is centrally concerned with establishing equality of material production and consumption among humans (at least those who survive the revolution). Another influence is the *progressive social reform movement* of early-twentieth-century urban America, in the tradition of Jane Addams, Lillian Wald, and Margaret Sanger, along with Social Gospel activists like Richard Ely and Walter Rauschenbusch—the primordial soup out of which American sociology as a professional discipline evolved—that identified, publicized, and sought through rational and philanthropic social amelioration to correct many social ills.[13] A somewhat related influence on American sociology's spiritual project is *American pragmatism*, of the John Dewey variety, which disavows metaphysics, takes liberal democracy (or whatever else a community happens to desire) for granted, and focuses on the piecemeal solving of immediate, practical problems, however people define them. Another influence on American sociology's spiritual project is a *therapeutic outlook and culture*—focused on individual subjective happiness, good feeling, and affirmation—received from the Freudian tradition of psychodynamics as mediated through twentieth-century psychoanalysis, pop psychology,

bringing together and extending the knowledge and insights of all the other (conceptually more restricted) adjacent disciplines." Gordon Marshall, 1998, *A Dictionary of Sociology*, 2nd ed., New York, Oxford University Press, p. 630.

13. Cecil Greek, 1992, *The Religious Roots of American Sociology*, New York: Garland; Dorothy Ross, 1991, *The Origins of American Social Science*, Cambridge: Cambridge University Press. See Christopher Lasch, 1991, *The True and Only Heaven: Progress and Its Critics*, New York: Norton; Ellen Fitzpatrick, 1994, *Endless Crusade: Women Social Scientists and Progressive Reform*, New York: Oxford University Press.

and advertisement-driven mass-consumer capitalism.[14] Still another formative influence on sociology's spiritual project is the *sexual revolution* of the 1960s and after, which has defined sexuality as a crucially determinative aspect of human personhood, identity, and agency, worthy of unbounded enjoyment and requiring political activism to protect and defend.

Added to these are the strong influences of the *black civil rights movement* of the 1950s and 60s and the *third-wave feminism* of the 1960s and 70s. More recently (1980s to the present), the cultural and political movement for *gay-lesbian-bisexual-transsexual-(gender/sexual)questioning (GLBTQ)* rights has exerted a massive impact on American sociology's spiritual project, viewed as naturally following the two previous influences of black civil rights and feminism. In more theoretical terms, the spiritual project of American sociology is also profoundly shaped by *social constructionism*, an outlook born in Kantian philosophy, bolstered by early Anthropology's arguments about cultural relativism, encouraged by a particular (mis)reading of Ludwig Wittgenstein's philosophy, and finally codified by sociology's very own Peter Berger and Thomas Luckmann (although Berger himself repudiated the "constructivist" movement that subsequently developed).[15] The pervasive influence of social constructionism as a defining worldview within sociology, even among the many who do not "do" the "social construction of social problems," cannot be underestimated. Finally, *poststructuralism* and *postmodernism* have exerted more diffuse but not insignificant influences on sociology's spiritual project. Most American sociologists are not disciples of Michel Foucault, Jacques Derrida,

---

14. Philip Rieff, *The Triumph of the Therapeutic: Uses of Faith after Freud*, New York: Harper and Row; Jonathan Imber, ed., 2004, *Therapeutic Culture*, New Brunswick: Transaction.

15. Peter Berger and Thomas Luckmann, 1967, *The Social Construction of Reality: A Treatise in the Sociology of Knowledge*, New York: Anchor Cite.

and Stanley Fish (as many in the humanities have been), but some of the sensibilities of poststructuralism and postmodernism—a detached skepticism about human subjectivity, authorial intent, disinterested knowledge, legitimate uses of power, and western humanism—have nevertheless diffused in sectors of American sociology in ways that shape its project.

If we had to characterize American sociology's sacred project in brief, therefore, we might say that it stands in the *modern liberal-Enlightenment-Marxist-social-reformist-pragmatist-therapeutic-sexually liberated-civil rights-feminist-GLBTQ-social constructionist-poststructuralist/postmodernist* "tradition." That odd conglomeration, I suggest, conveys much of the lineage, interest, and energy propelling the spiritual project of American sociology. Again, it does not matter that this or that particular important sociologist is or is not aware of or does or does not believe in or endorse all of the elements of or influences on this spiritual project. What matters is that it in fact animates, though not necessarily consciously and explicitly, the working beliefs and activities of many if not most American sociologists, especially those who are most vocal and activist, and so has come to define the presupposed, default, "obvious" purpose, culture, and institutional orientation of the discipline. In fact, the more that the features of this sacred project are simply assumed, tacit, and unnoticed by its adherents, the more powerfully they can and do operate among sociologists.

I should say here that I personally do not view this sacred project as all bad or all good; in my view, it is a mix of both. But my personal view on that is not what matters most here. I am interested in writing neither a diatribe against nor a manifesto championing this sacred project. My purpose is more simply to name and describe it for what it is and to critically consider some of its larger ramifications. It is less important how sociology's sacred project does or does not match my own personal standards and sensibilities. What matters is helping readers to see and acknowledge its reality and influences, and to consider their larger implications and consequences for sociology and beyond.

That said, let me unpack American sociology's dominant sacred project a bit more. This project is, first, intent to *realize* an end. It is going somewhere. It is fundamentally teleological, oriented toward a final goal. It is not about defending or conserving a received inheritance, but unsettling the status quo. The project is fundamentally transformational, reformist, sometimes revolutionary. It is about "changing the world" to "make the world a better place." The change that sociology's sacred project seeks to effect is also dramatic. The problems of the social world are so big and deep in this view that mere remedial tinkering or prudent meliorism is inadequate. Change needs to be systemic, institutional, and sometimes radical—in the etymological sense of "going to the root" of things.[16] So when the new world envisioned by this spiritual project is finally realized, it will be very different from the present world.

And how will this be accomplished? Through various means, but central among them in sociology's spiritual imagination are popular progressive social movements and social-democratic state programs and regulations.[17] "The people" (on the left, not the middle and definitely not the right) must demand justice and equality, and then the state must guarantee and accomplish justice and equality

16. Etymologically, "radical," late fourteenth century, from Late Latin *radicalis*, "of or having roots," from Latin *radix*, "root."

17. For one explicit statement about the need to unite sociology and progressive activism, see the chapters on "Scholarship that Might Matter," "Crossing Boundaries in Participatory Action Research: Performing Protest with Drag Queens," "Building Bridges, Building Leaders: Theory, Action, and Lived Experience," "Knowing What's Wrong is Not Enough: Creating Vision and Strategy," among others, in David Croteau, William Hoynes, and Charlotte Ryan, *Rhyming Hope and History: Activists, Academics, and Social Movement Scholarship* (Minneapolis: University of Minnesota Press, 2005), which explicitly seeks to promote "partnerships among scholars and activists" for "meaningful collaboration" (back cover).

"structurally" through progressive programs and policies. The market, wealthy elites, charitable foundations, moral leaders, and religious organizations are not to be trusted to achieve the goods that sociology prizes—most of those, in fact, are often viewed as sources of the world's current problems. In general, the wealth of capitalists needs to be redistributed, and the world would be a better place if it were much more secular. So, in the end, most ordinary people cannot be trusted (because they do not "get it"), nor can established institutions and their leaders be trusted. So those who *do* "get it"—who have a "sociological imagination"—must (somehow) compel the state to socially structure equality, freedom, and justice for all, especially those against whom mainstream society would discriminate.

Emancipation thus also centrally defines sociology's sacred project. People need to be set free from everything external that oppresses, constrains, and dehumanizes them, whether that takes the form of ignorance, racism, poverty, patriarchy, heterosexism, or any other discrimination or obstruction, perhaps including the institutions of marriage and religion. Thus the archetypically modern devotion to freedom, to *liberté*, is generalized in this project. A key substantive commitment in sociology's sacred project is also *equality*. Nobody is any better or more valuable or important than anyone else. Everyone deserves an equal opportunity for—and probably even an equal outcome in—enjoying material goods and social respect. Significant privileges, status distinctions, and categories of discrimination are therefore bads to be targeted for destruction.

To the more traditional western commitments to freedom and equality, sociology's sacred project also adds the centrality of *moral affirmation*. In some ways, this is contemporary American society's version of the French Revolution's ideal of *fraternité*. It is not, for this project, enough simply to set people free from oppression and to treat them as equals. Everyone also deserves to be morally affirmed by everyone else in their society. Justice and equity are not sufficient: it is necessary to ensure the kind of social and moral approval, validation, appreciation, and approbation that people are believed to need to feel good about themselves. Unacceptable, therefore, is any form of real or symbolic lack of acceptance, exclusion, or moral judgment against another. Every identity and lifestyle must be not only tolerated but positively validated, affirmed, and included.

The focal concern of sociology's sacred project is the welfare of *human beings*. Many sociologists are also concerned about the welfare of the natural environment and animals. However, with some exceptions, it is about the rights and well-being of humanity that this sacred project is most concerned—but *humanity understood in a very particular way*. A *highly specific philosophical anthropology* is at work here. First, human beings are believed to be (or at least should be) *autonomous*. This may seem strange for a discipline devoted to showing how individual people are powerfully influenced, if not constituted and determined, by their social environments. But sociology's sacred project finds a way to finesse this tension. The controlling influencer that society is, which sociology reveals, is associated with the constraining (oppressive, exploiting, discriminating) part of human experience, which the individual needs to resist and overcome if he or she is to be free, happy, and healthy.[18] The individual human person, then, is understood as naturally, and thus ideally, autonomous—as a distinct agent (that should be) in charge of its own body, self, decisions, and destiny. The crucial disciplinary contribution to its own project is thus for sociology to discover and expose the many unjust and oppressive ways that "society"

18. This "homo-duplex" model of individual-versus-society was the common assumption of sociology's founding fathers—see Christian Smith, 2015, *To Flourish or Destruct: A Personalist Theory of Human Goods, Motivations, Failure, and Evil*, Chicago: University of Chicago Press; also see Jonathan Fish, 2013, "Homo Duplex Revisited: A Defense of Emile Durkheim's Theory of Moral Self," *Journal of Classical Sociology*, May 31, pp. 1–21.

constraints, exploits, and oppresses individuals, so that they can be challenged and surmounted. "The social" is thus construed as essential to humanity's problem, an all-too-often dehumanizing force that must be subverted and reconstructed to foster individuals' autonomy.

Human beings ought also, in this view, to be *self-directing*. People should not be controlled or commanded by anyone but themselves. The direction of action for each person must come from the will of each person. Whatever happens by, with, and to any given person should be determined by that person, and nothing or nobody else. In this vision, human persons are obviously most authentically and rightfully *individuals*. People are not cells of a social body, dwellers on a Great Chain of Being, or subjects of Kingdom, Church, or Nation. All people of course need to be—as sociology as a project itself is—enlightened and converted and made part of the collective movement animated by this sacred project. But the movement itself must never violate anyone's individuality, for that would itself violate the vision and commitment of the movement. Solidarity, in short, is instrumental and contractual, not ontological and encumbering. Individuals, by this account, are also conceived of as *agents*. This means they possess "agency." Individuals are not fundamentally objects on which other forces act but the subjects of action and interaction of which they themselves are the efficient causes. They thus are and rightly ought to be the capable, empowered, authorized actors who make things happen in the world and in their own lives.

What, then, according to this sacred project, are these emancipated, equal, morally affirmed, autonomous, self-directed, individual agents to be doing with their individual freedom, equality, affirmation, and autonomy? They *should be* acting *to live their lives as they so desire*. Here the descriptive and the normative combine. Humans are believed to be creatures both who naturally seek to live as they desire (the descriptive) and who ought to live as they so desire (the normative). The teleological end in this point follows naturally from the philosophical-anthropology and moral commitments to individual emancipation, autonomy, self-direction, agency, and moral affirmation, as described above. People have lives to live, and the best lives for them are those lived according to the desires generated by each individual's interests and wishes. The good world envisioned by this sacred project, therefore, is one in which each individual is free to live as he or she so desires—so long, to recite the standard rule, as they do not prevent any other individual from doing the same.

But does this sacred vision provide any more substantive content to what a good human life is likely to be, how individuals should capitalize upon their freedom and equality? Yes. Three somewhat substantive focuses help to define good human ends here. One involves individuals *constructing their own favored identities.* The question concerns who people are, in their own self-understanding and in the way others understand them. Identities define people and form their experiences. So each person needs to be able to construct his or her own identity in ways that fit their self-determined desires in life. Inherited and ascribed identities of family, religion, race, ethnicity, town, occupation, sexual orientation, and so on may not fit individual desires, so must be ready to be cast off or reconstructed. This of course requires an openness and fluidity in self-understanding. It also requires proficiency in the manipulation of symbolic markers of identity—styles of clothing, language, hair style and color, bodily inscriptions (tattoos, etc.), and so on—in order to achieve the desired self-presentation and affirmation. In any case, no other person or institution should be able to tell anyone who and what she or he is. That is a matter for each individual to decide, create, and express for herself or himself.

Two other somewhat substantive features of the individually self-directed good life envisioned by American sociology's spiritual project are freedom to *enter and exit relationships as they choose* and *to equally enjoy the gratification of experiential, material, and bodily pleasures.* The underlying logic is the same as concerning identity construction. A good part of the best in human life consists in consuming stimulating experiences, relationships, material goods, and bodily pleasures. Each individual should be free to do so in a way that satisfies her or his own self-determined desires and will, and all people should have equal access to those goods. An equitable distribution of experiences and material goods is needed for people to live good lives. And people should be free to engage in any relationship they should so choose. The same applies to the enjoyment of other forms of pleasurable experiences. Since different people find different kinds of experiences to be pleasurable, nobody has the right to define what pleasures or relationships other people should pursue and enjoy. A good life and society throws off the restrictive, repressive constraints placed on the gratification of individual pleasures and frees everyone to satisfy any pleasure that she or he so desires—provided, again, that doing so does not interfere with anyone else being able to do the same (which is ensured by informal contractual engagements by countless exchanges of informed consent among adults[19]). And if any people go public with the particular forms of pleasure or relationships that most please them, everyone else ought to accept them and ideally morally affirm their personal preferences and choices.

That is American sociology's sacred project. Some sociologists may disagree or wish to revise my formulation of the issue. All of it is a matter open for discussion, my side of which I develop and substantiate below. But if I am anything close to correct in my description here, it is clear that sociology is certainly more than "the

---

19. Children are much more difficult to fit into this picture, for multiple reasons—as they are generally in liberal theory.

scientific study of society." It is, rather, caught up in a major endeavor of (what is understood and experienced by those committed to it) a valiant moral cause of profound human meaning, ultimate personal value, and world-historical importance that defines the ultimate horizons of vision, purpose, and devotion.[20]

REFLECTIONS, QUALIFICATIONS, AND TENSIONS

Worth noting, at this point, as an aside, is how closely sociology's sacred, spiritual project parallels that of (especially Protestant) Christianity in its structure of beliefs, interests, and expectations. It would not be wrong to say that sociology's project represents essentially a secularized version of the Christian gospel and worldview. Both are teleological, seeing history as going somewhere of ultimate importance. Both look toward an eventual dramatic transformation of the world in a way that is also importantly linked to smaller transformations in the lives of converted believers here and now. Both view the basic problem as a kind of bondage to some form of "evil," from which humans need to be set free. Both understand that something more than individual effort is needed to effect the liberation of humans from evil. Both take seriously an essential equality of human persons when it comes to their most important social relations, whether they be to God or other humans. Both grasp the central importance of something like the unique value and dignity of

---

20. Sociological readers, at least, should fully understand what I mean by "sacred" and how it arguably applies to sociology's project. As to the word "spiritual," if readers still object to my use of that term here, then I say temporary replace the phrase "spiritual project" with "social movement driven from deep within the human spirit," and then read on and see if my argument proves persuasive in the end. Even if the term "spiritual" ends up being a point of contention, the rest of my substantive argument still stands and must be engaged. And in any case, "sacred" holds up perfectly well in my argument.

each distinct human life—that no person or class of people is simply expendable. Both emphasize moral responsibility to take care of the poor and needy.[21] Both understand the importance of the need for human moral affirmation, of "justification." American sociology's sacred project's emphasis on human autonomy, self-direction, and agency parallels Christianity's teachings on humanity's absolute ontological distinction from God, capacity for meaningful free will, and the moral responsibility to make righteous and obedient choices.[22] Both repudiate absolutely deterministic, relativistic, and nihilistic views of reality and human action. Both also understand the tight connection between what humans *are* and how humans *ought* to live, between the descriptive and the prescriptive in human existence. Sociology's sacred project's emphasis on free identity (re)

21. Many sociologists do not know—mostly because they subscribe to various ill-informed prejudices against and stereotypes about it—the powerful ethical impulses that exist within the Christian tradition not only encouraging "giving alms" to the poor but also to work toward and for the elimination of poverty, human equality, healing of the sick, and gender egalitarianism, impulses that recurrently surge up in the tradition, even when many Christians also recurrently fail to realize those ethical impulses and more than a few actively work against them. See, among the massive literature, Mary Malone, 2001, *Women and Christianity*, Maryknoll, NY: Orbis Books; Donal Dorr, 1992, *Option for the Poor*, Maryknoll, NY: Orbis Books; Rodney Stark, 1997, *The Rise of Christianity: A Sociologist Reconsiders History*, Princeton: Princeton University Press; Craig Blomberg, 1999, *Neither Povery Nor Riches*, Grand Rapids: Eerdmans; Patricia Ranft, 2000, *Women and Spiritual Equality in Christian Tradition*, New York: Palgrave Macmillan; in Christian scripture, see, for just a sample, Matthew 19:21, Matthew 25:40, 2 Corintians 8:13–14, Ephesians 5:21, and James 5:1. The philosopher Charles Taylor's intriguing thesis, in fact, is that secular modernity is at heart a championing of Christian social ethics in secular terms, a task taken up because those social ethics were and are so compelling yet Christendom too much failed to achieve them within its own religious institutional framework (Taylor, 1999, "A Catholic Modernity?," in James Heft, ed., *A Catholic Modernity?*, New York: Oxford University Press, pp. 13–37).

22. A fascinating history connects secular modernity's valorizing of autonomous individual choice back to the influential late-medieval theological nominalist's absolutely sovereign, volition-centered view of God, advanced by thinkers such as William of Ockham and his followers—in which, as history unfolds, eventually the sovereign God is replaced by willful humans. See Michael Gillespie, 2008, *The Theological Origins of Modernity*, 2008, Chicago: University of Chicago Press; William Placher, 1996, *The Domestication of Transcendence*, Louisville: Westminster John Knox.

construction also closely mirrors Christianity's belief in personal conversion, sanctification, and moral transformation. And sociology's interest in satisfying experiential and material consumptions and in gratifying pleasures approximate Christian teachings on the goodness of creation and the body, God's gift of creation to humanity, and the gospel's promise of abundant life, the heavenly banquet, and eternal bliss in beatitude with God. Last but not least, both are committed to spreading "good news," as they see it, among those who are lost in darkness.

Broadly speaking, in fact, American sociology's sacred project is a secular salvation story developed out of the modern traditions of Enlightenment, liberalism, Marxism, reformist progressivism, pragmatism, therapeutic culture, sexual liberation, civil rights, feminism, and so on. It is as if, standing within the secular modern movement that had jettisoned the Christianity and Judaism that had so shaped the western imagination for two millennia, and so demystified the world, American sociologists felt compelled to fill in the sacred and eschatological void left in Christianity and Judaism's absence by constructing, embracing, and proselytizing the world with a secular salvation gospel of its own making. Or perhaps this was not an "as if" situation, but what actually happened. This is yet another way that sociology's project is ultimately *spiritual* and sacred, and not simply political or ideological.

I want to emphasize this last point. The categories of "political," "ideological," or even "moral" alone are inadequate for describing the kind of visions to which I am saying American sociology is committed.[23] If these other categories were sufficient, then the

---

23. Anxious discussions about sociology being too liberal, leftist, or politicized have been recurrent in the discipline—see, for example, Stephen Cole, 1994, "Why Sociology Doesn't Make Progress like the Natural Sciences," *Sociological Forum*, 9: 133–154; James Davis, 1994, "What's Wrong with Sociology?," *Sociological Forum*, 9: 179–197; Randall Collins, 1994, "Why the Social Sciences Won't Become High-Consensus,

significance of my analysis would deflate. I would be reduced to observing merely that sociology faculty tend to be composed of a certain political type, that sociology has a certain ideological bent, or that sociologists are motivated by certain moral commitments. Those observations are true, but not new or insightful. More significant is the fact that, above and beyond these more common observations, sociology is in fact committed to a particular *project* that is deeply *sacred* in nature. If sociology's project was merely political, then it would only concern a restructuring of power relations. If sociology's interests were simply ideological, then we would be dealing in a more limited way with a value- and interest-laden system of ideas. And if what I am describing here was only about a set of moral beliefs, then the issues involved would be limited to mere judgments about right and wrong, good and bad, and so on. But American sociology and its concerns are about much more than that. Also incomplete and misleading would be to say merely that sociology is dedicated to "improving the human condition" or to "human welfare." Those vaguely philanthropic expressions sound nice but lack much particular content specifying what is wrong with the human situation that needs improving and what the human good is that defines an enhancement of its well-being. On those points, sociology's sacred project has a much more

Rapid-Discovery Science," *Sociological Forum*, 9: 155–177; Seymour Martin Lipset, 1994, "The State of American Sociology," *Sociological Forum*, 9: 199–220; Harvey Molotch, 1994, "Going Out," *Sociological Forum*, 9: 221–239; Arthur Stinchcombe, 1994, "Disintegrated Disciplines and the Future of Sociology," *Sociological Forum*, 9: 279–291; summarized with other chapters in Stephen Cole, 2001, *What is Wrong with Sociology?*, New Brunswick, NJ: Transaction; http ://www.mindingthecampus.com/originals/2010/10/imber.html,http://orgtheory.wordpress.com/2007/07/19/why-does-sociology-have-such-a-bad-reputation/, http://orgtheory.wordpress.com/2010/11/05/sociology-is-doing-ok/, http://www.coordinationproblem.org/2010/10/the-forty-year-failure-of-american-sociology.html; Imber, 1999. Even if the issue was merely political, there would still be very good grounds to justify a discussion about whether sociology really is or should be essentially the criminal investigation unit of the left wing of the Democratic Party.

substantively specific, robust, and visionary take on the problems and solutions.

But can we really believe that American sociology is at heart a spiritual project, a Durkheimian sacred? That seems so incongruous. Pondering the counterfactual case, I suggest, helps to bring the spiritual nature of American sociology's project into starker relief. Imagine this (if possible): What if sociology really and truly was nothing but a purely scientific, objectively neutral, spiritually disinterested, just-the-facts-and-theory study of society? Would most current-day sociologists really want to be a part of it? How would it be different than it is now? For one thing, sociology departments would have far fewer undergraduate majors and graduate students than they currently have. Sociology of that kind just wouldn't be that attractive to as many students. For another thing, the undergraduate and graduate students that sociology would attract would be a very different bunch of people than they are now, ideologically, culturally, and politically. The composition of its practitioners would be more blandly mainstream, facts-oriented, and technocratic. Furthermore, the subject matter of the journal articles and the content and tone of the books that such a spiritually blank sociology would produce would also be very different than they are now (as described below). The unholy trinity of race, class, and gender, for example, would take a demoted place among a host of other, less morally fraught interests and concerns. Sociologists would generally be less impassioned about their work, and they would enter their classrooms with less of an agenda to convince and transform their students. Overall, sociology would be less "theoretical," more dedicated to "bean counting," less inspiring, more boring. That is exactly what worlds lacking sacred, spiritual vision and purpose tend to become: collections of humdrum empirical facts and experiences. The fact that American sociology is *not* that indicates yet again how very *spiritual* (in the sense that I mean that) its energizing *project* actually is.

I must also repeat that I am not claiming that all American sociologists are personally committed to their discipline's sacred project. Most are, I think, being more or less conscious and activist on behalf of it. But some are not. A minority of sociologists are believers in sociology as purely a scientific study of society; many of these lean toward a neo-positivist approach. They care mostly about good methods, improving measures, closely matching data and theory, the mathematics behind statistics, careful analysis, high standards for publication, and the best training of the next generation of sociologists. I have known some of these and they are often very fine people. They can get annoyed at the more dominant, activist sacred disciples in the discipline, but they are not "political" enough to take them on. Mostly they simply try instead to "keep their own shops clean" and set reasonable boundaries in their programs. These kinds of sociologists do have an influence in the discipline, but they do not dominate its culture any more than Mormons dominate American religious culture.

Other kinds of sociologists are likewise not personally committed to sociology's sacred project, but similarly do not define the discipline's culture. Some are just commonplace "institution improvers," conducting institutional research to try to help hospitals and correctional systems, for instance, be more effective. Others are professional data collectors, working for government agencies— such as the Census Bureau—or for-profit research firms. Yet others are ordinary, middle-America college professors who simply like to learn and teach about the family, criminal justice, or what have you. Here and there American sociologists are evangelical Protestants, conservative Catholics, moderate mainline Protestants, and Mormons, and find sociology's sacred project difficult to buy into. And a few others are true old-school liberals who genuinely believe in toler-ance, fairness, and pluralism all the way down, and who recognize in certain more zealous aspects of sociology's spiritual project tenden-cies toward totalitarianism (they still remember the mid-twentieth century). All of these other positions exist in American sociology. But, again, none of them determines its center of gravity. None de-fines the dominant culture. None of them possesses the numbers or positions to be able to control the prevailing assumptions, ethos, and discourse. Consequently, any given person objecting to my story on the grounds that she or he knows sociologists not representing the sacred project I am describing here misses the mark. Again, I am not talking about this or that individual sociologist or even small network of sociologists; I am talking about the discipline's *dominant* culture, sensibilities, interests, discourse, and project.

It should be noted, too, that sociology's sacred project is not monolithic in its expression, even among those committed to it. There is variance in ways American sociologists pursue it. Some are "true believers" who wear it on their sleeves and revel in being activists who promote it at every possible opportunity.[24] If I had to guess, I would say that true believers represent 30 to 40 percent of American sociologists. Others are essentially on board, but are more circumspect in how they express it. These I would guess ac-count for between 50 and 60 percent of sociologists. Some sociolo-gists endorse a radical revolutionary version of the sacred project. These are true apostles out to "turn the world upside down." Others prefer the more moderate, liberal approach that fits more easily into mainstream politics and sophisticated, urbane, cultural life (and

24. To be sure, however, even many among the true believers have not thought through the intellectual foundations of their project or cannot articulate it in a way that I have tried to rationally reconstruct it here. Very many are going on confident intuitive sensibili-ties and gut instincts that have been cultivated by formative influences earlier in their lives and are sustained at present through the plausibility structures that the profession of sociology affords.

academic privilege). Some emphasize the Marxist or feminist or gay-rights aspects of the project. Others cast it in more utilitarian, rational-choice terms. Still others pursue the project on particularly Durkheimian, Bourdieusian, or Goffmanesque footings. So, from *within* sociology's sacred project, it can often look as if major differences divide those who I am saying are its adherents, when in fact their differences are relatively small compared to the genuine alternatives—just as within Islam, for example, differences among Sunnis, Shia, Sufis, and other minority groups can look huge from within but much less so when compared from without to other religions. Most sociologists, despite their apparent differences, share an underlying commitment—however self-consciously so or not—to the larger spiritual project. Even some of the more aloof, detached, analytical, and scientistic of American sociologists tend, when scratched hard enough, to show their true colors as *sympathizers*, if not believers in the project too. They may operate with a different professional style, but when it comes to possible threats to the sacred project, they usually come out as invested in its sacred vision like the rest. In brief, American sociology affords a variety of ways for individual sociologists to engage and promote its sacred project (which of course the project itself demands), but the deep, underlying vision and purpose in which they are so variously engaged is in fact quite similar and shared across the more surface differences.

We should also recognize that the sacred project of American sociology, being such an amalgam of various cultural and political concerns and agendas described above (liberal-Enlightenment-Marxist-reformist-pragmatist-therapeutic-sexually liberated-civil rights-feminist-GLBTQ-social constructionist-poststructuralist/postmodernist), comprises more than a few internal tensions and contradictions. For example, American sociology's sacred project is deeply bought into the relativizing power of social constructionism as an essential doctrine, yet the very validity of its project also depends upon sociology telling the world about the *true* facts about the way reality *really* is. To believe on strong social-constructionist grounds that everything is ultimately culturally-cognitively-morally relative cuts the legs out from under the serious imperative of sociology's spiritual project; yet to instead take a strong realist stand about the way social reality really is and works starts to place reality-based constraints on the heady autonomy, emancipation, self-construction, and self-direction that its sacred project presupposes and champions.

Parallel to this tension is the question of the seemingly privileged place of sociology in any system of human knowledge production. Sociology, in pursuing its sacred purposes, recurrently debunks the human social world as something quite different than what it seems to be. Behind ordinary social appearances lurk labyrinths of conflicting relations of interest, power, control, resource flows, habitus, and so on that ought to make us question the world as given to us. But if this is true, then how does that not also apply to sociology itself? Why should we trust sociology to tell us the reliable truth any more than any other human social institution or tradition? On what grounds is sociology uniquely immune from the debunking powers of its own method? At this point, the "sociology-is-the-*science*-of-social-life" claim is usually trotted out, as if simply making asserting that "sociology is scientific" somehow removes it from the epistemologically corrosive acids of its own skeptical perspective. Whether or not that works in any particular case is beside the point. Sociology's position of being a debunking discipline whose disciplinary authority depends upon it remaining immune from being debunked is inevitably fraught with tensions, if not self-defeating contradictions.

Another example: Sociology and its sacred project embody a strong populist and egalitarian streak, on the one hand, yet simultaneously an elitist outlook, on the other. Salvation is given for all, so to speak, but only the sociologically enlightened and converted are the elect children of light, locked in righteous struggle against the children of darkness. In this, a wide embrace for all common people (represented by, say, Dr. Martin Luther King, Jr.) coexists uneasily in sociology's sacred project with a narrow trust placed in only the most highly committed vanguard (think here of V. I. Lenin). Democracy is valued insofar as it gives "the people" a chance to force greater justice and equality on the rich and powerful; unfortunately, however, most of "the people" themselves cannot be trusted to know and demand the correct things (given their false consciousness promoted by mass-consumer advertising, non-progressive religion, lack of sociological education, and other insidious influences), so mobilizing progressive coalitions, while undermining unenlightened, "red-state" middle Americans, "fundamentalists," right-wingers, and other benighted oafs, is crucial. Eventually, most people will have to see the light. In such ways, American sociology's genuinely egalitarian sensibilities inevitably run up against its also-very-real disciplinary gnostic elitism, in which those relatively few who "get it" are happily inducted as the enlightened ones belonging to a quasi-secret society, and the rest are treated with an irritated roll of the eyes and sometimes outright scorn as the "ordinary ignorant."[25]

---

25. This attitude is ubiquitous in American sociology, but it is worth providing one illustration of it here. In his attempt to answer the question "what is wrong with American sociology?," Harvey Molotch with some defensiveness replied, "We are misfits. The most developed sociology in the world exists in a country inhospitable to it. The related US traits of individualism, jingoistic arrogance, and lack of a labor party tradition combine to make sociology a suspect endeavor. There is little incentive [for others] to understand our underlying assumptions nor attend to the progress of our work. The ideas of social structure, of social facts, of situated behavior are hard sells in a land where the way to get elected, to become head of the PTA, or make a living in consulting is by pushing wars on drugs and locking people up. Our national traditions support forms of making sense that run counter to ours. Absent a strong hunch that social conditions affect individual behavior, you get a blameful and dangerous society and certainly one with little use for sociology" (1996: 221). For a broad critique of such an approach, see Lasch 1991.

Chapter 2

Evidence

Readers may grant that my thesis is intriguing. But does empirical evidence substantiate it? I think so, although the evidence I can offer is not "conclusive," at least when the standards of proof are set as the types that count for, say, publication in top journals. The existence and influence of sacred projects that operate beneath the surface and among people living somewhat in denial about their true nature are not readily proven with survey or interview data. What is actually most personally convincing about such ideas is the experience of many years spent in American sociology, viewed with an open but critical eye from both the inside and the outside. I have learned and taught sociology in a small liberal arts college, at a major private Ivy League university, in a major public research university, and at another elite, private university. While I usually felt at home in these settings, for various reasons I also always felt some distance from and marginality in relation to American sociology. Thirty years of curious personal experience in that kind of position has led me to the argument I advance here. I am hopeful that, if I make my case, enough others will intuitively grasp the truth of my thesis, based on their own personal experience and observations.

Still, one or another person's experience does not convincing evidence make. So what other evidence might I marshal to support my case? Again, there is no practical way to directly "test" my thesis with standard sociological measures; the issues involved are too subtle and elusive to be "verified" by such means. I will, however, offer an array of semi-systematic evidence to try to render my thesis comprehensible and plausible.

A STROLL THROUGH THE ASA'S ANNUAL CONVENTION BOOK EXHIBIT

Books are a great place to start. I love books. So, one of my favorite parts of the annual ASA national meetings—besides visiting with old friends and colleagues—is browsing through the sociology book exhibits that each year occupy some cavernous convention space down in the bowels of the meeting's convention center. Having paid my $295 to register for the meeting, I am able with my registration ID to pass the security staff who police the book exhibit entrance (presumably to prevent mobs of unregistered sneaks from illicitly enjoying looking at the new and recently published books). Inside, the seemingly endless displays of sociology monographs and textbooks by nearly every university and trade press imaginable is overwhelming. My first reaction is often despair over the number of interesting and important books that I know I will never have the time to read. The range of topics, genres, methods, and stories is vast and exciting.

After some time spent browsing the host of books on display, however, some similarities and patterns among them begin to emerge. What most of these sociology books are about, in fact, starts to look increasingly less diverse and actually more repetitive. Then, through a process of "grounded theory" development—by which sociologists usually mean simply looking at the world as it is without too many predetermined ideas and trying to make some sense of it—certain typifying categories start to emerge. With them in mind and additional perusing of the wares for sale, one realizes that most of the books that sociology is producing and consuming are actually about only a relatively small number of concerns and themes. In fact, one realizes, most of their specific titles could be translated into more generic forms, as follows:

- *People are Not Paying Enough Attention to Social Problem X, But if They Read this Book they Will Realize that They Have To*
- *Women, Racial Minorities, and Poor People are Horribly Oppressed and You Should Be Really Angry about That!*
- *See How the System Run by the Rich Obstructs Justice?*
- *Gays, Lesbians, Transsexuals, and other Queers are Everywhere and Their Experiences are Some of the Most Important Things Ever to Know About*
- *Public Education Today is Falling Apart and Here is Why*
- *Home Schoolers and Private Religious Schoolers are Weird and Depriving Other Children of their Rights to Equal Education*
- *Popular Social Movements that Challenge the Unjust Status Quo are Really Cool*
- *Anything But the Most Liberal Religion is Violent, Fanatical, and Scary*
- *Everything You Think is Real is Actually a Social Construction Fomented by Devious Hegemonic Powers in Order to Subjugate and Exploit the Rest of Us*
- *Sex Workers, Drug Addicts, Antisocial Youth, Mass Murderers, and Other "Deviants" Are Actually Among the Most Normal People Out There if You Just Get to Know Them*

- *Neo-Liberal Capitalism is the Most Evil, Destructive Force on Earth*
- *Social Structures Determine Life, But Individual Agency is Really Important Too!*

I am not making (too much) fun of this; this is just the way it is. (I can also testify that three years of experience as book review editor for the journal *Social Forces*, which required me to examine oceans of sociology books sent in by myriad publishers, both great and lowly, confirms this analysis exactly.) I actually think that a lot of such books have many true, important, and interesting things to say; in fact, I have published more than a few of just these kinds of books myself.[1] But, in whatever way one evaluates them, the empirical fact stands that these are the kinds of works representing the majority of sociology books being published. There are not a lot of books in sociology that take any significantly different perspective. Only on occasion are these typical kinds of titles on display at the ASA convention punctuated by quite different (more tedious) book titles, like:

- *Multinomial Polychoric Methods for the Imputation of Non-Parametrically Missing Trace Data in Clustered Urban Samples*

and

- *Explaining 1 Percent of the Variance in Child Prevention Practices of the Muslim–Buddhist Minority Residents of Timbuktu Who are Employed in the Nascent Service Sector*

1. For example, Smith, 1996, *Resisting Reagan: The U.S. Central America Peace Movement*, Chicago: University of Chicago Press; Smith, 2010, *Lost in Transition: The Dark Side of Emerging Adulthood*, New York: Oxford University Press; Michael O. Emerson and Christian Smith, 2001, *Divided by Faith: Religion and the Problem of Race in America*, New York: Oxford University Press.

Otherwise, the standard fare is mostly about the kind of titles named in generic form above. To show that I am not fibbing, here are some actual titles of books found on display in the ASA book exhibit:

- *The Price of Paradise: The Costs of Inequality and a Vision for a More Equitable America*
- *The Industrial Diet: The Degradation of Food and the Struggle for Healthy Eating*
- *Living Out Islam: Voices of Gay, Lesbian, and Transgender Muslims*
- *Cut It Out: The C-Section Epidemic in America*
- *22 Ideas to Fix the World: Conversations with the World's Foremost Thinkers*
- *Rhetorics of Insecurity: Belonging and Violence in the Neoliberal Era*
- *Breaking Women: Gender, Race, and the New Politics of Imprisonment*
- *Pagan Family Values: Childhood and the Religious Imagination in Contemporary American Paganism*
- *Is Breast Best?: Taking on the Breastfeeding Experts and the New High Stakes of Motherhood*
- *Buying into Fair Trade: Culture, Morality, and Consumption*
- *Up Against a Wall: Rape Reform and the Failure of Success*
- *The New Kinship: Constructing Donor-Conceived Families*
- *Respect Yourself, Protect Yourself: Latina Girls and Sexual Identity*
- *Blacks and Whites in Christian America: How Racial Discrimination Shapes Religious Convictions*
- *Pray the Gay Away: The Extraordinary Lives of Bible Belt Gays*

- *Gun Crusaders: The NRA's Culture War*
- *The Gender Trap: Parents and the Pitfalls of Raising Boys and Girls*
- *Homeroom Security: School Discipline in an Age of Fear*
- *Not My Kid: What Parents Believe about the Sex Lives of Their Teenagers*
- *The Wrong Complexion for Protection: How the Government Response to Disaster Endangers African American Communities*
- *The Hip-Hop Generation Fights Back: Youth, Activism and Post-Civil Rights Politics*
- *Killing McVeigh: The Death Penalty and the Myth of Closure*
- *Arrested Justice: Black Women, Violence, and America's Prison Nation*
- *One Marriage Under God: The Campaign to Promote Marriage in America*
- *The Bully Society: School Shootings and the Crisis of Bullying in America's Schools*
- *Legalizing Prostitution: From Illicit Vice to Lawful Business*
- *Shutting Down the Streets: Political Violence and Social Control in the Global Era*
- *The Slums of Aspen: Immigrants vs. the Environment in America's Eden*
- *Entitled to Nothing: The Struggle for Immigrant Health Care in the Age of Welfare Reform*
- *The Tender Cut: Inside the Hidden World of Self-Injury*
- *Punished: Policing the Lives of Black and Latino Boys*
- *Street Kids: Homeless Youth, Outreach, and Policing New York's Streets*

Actually, these are merely some of the titles from the sociology list of *only one* university-press publisher, the first one at which I randomly happened to take a look. The other titles by this publisher not listed here are not very different either. For those of us who have carefully observed sociology book lists and conference-exhibit displays for many years, we know that a look at the sociology lists of virtually every other university press and trade publisher would produce a list very similar to the one above. Rather than dragging readers here through multiple similar lists of sociology titles that all demonstrate the same point, I invite anyone to look them up on any relevant publisher's website. She or he will find my argument here corroborated. One moderately careful scan of the titles themselves reveals the narrow range of themes and perspectives with which most sociologists are preoccupied.

I am quite sympathetic to many of the apparent concerns expressed in the titles of most (though not all) of these books. I do not draw attention to them because I think they are all wrong and should be stopped. I am not at all against them as specific books being published. What I *am* against—for reasons I will explain below—is American sociology being and actively promoting a particular sacred project while also living in denial about the real nature of that project and presenting itself instead to others as the mere "science of human social life." What *is* wrong is American sociology being packed full of like-minded scholars and teachers who do not fully own up to their discipline's shared spiritual project, despite the fact that they tend to produce mostly these type of books as activist disciples of that sacred project. So much for celebrating diversity, the proactive inclusion of social others, and welcoming differences. In American sociology, such things rarely actually happen, unless they somehow fit the narrow range of differences that the sacred project endorses. The ideology is there, but the institutionalized practices negate it.

EXEMPLARS

Let us note a handful of particular sociology books as exemplars of sociology's sacred project:

Going Solo: The Extraordinary Rise and Surprising Appeal of Living Alone (Penguin Books, 2012) by Eric Kleinenberg, New York University. This book not only describes and explains the empirical trends and people's experiences of living alone— rather than, say, getting married—but takes an informal normative position positively recommending the benefits of living alone. No wonder one Amazon.com reviewer writes, "This book really will change the lives of people who live solo, and everyone else. At least it should."

Gender Vertigo: American Families in Transition (Yale University Press, 1999) by Barbara Risman, University of Illinois Chicago. The book's self-description tells it all: "Risman . . . provides empirical evidence that human beings are capable of enduring and affective intimate relationships without gender as the central organizing mechanism. The data also strongly indicate that men and women are capable of changing gendered ways of being throughout their lives. In her analysis of nontraditional families, Risman finds that gender expectations can be overcome if couples are willing to flout society and risk 'gender vertigo.' . . . The author argues that we can create a just society only by creating a society in which gender is an irrelevant category for social life—a post-gender society."

Society without God: What the Least Religious Nations Can Tell Us About Contentment (New York University Press, 2010) by Phil Zuckerman, Pitzer College. Based on 150 convenience-sample interviews in Denmark and Sweden, the book counters the idea that "a society without God would be hell on earth"

(?) by showing that Danes and Swedes enjoy strong economies, low crime rates, high standards of living, and social equality, and seem to be very happy people. The book nicely promotes the view that "the world can be more peaceful without organized religion" (as one Amazon.com reviewer wrote). No wonder the New Atheist author/activist, Sam Harris, plugs this book, saying, "Zuckerman's research is truly indispensable." Just guess what Zuckerman's other book, *Faith No More: Why People Reject Religion* (Oxford University Press, 2011) has to say.

Risky Lessons: Sex Education and Social Inequality (Rutgers University Press, 2008) by Jessica Fields, San Francisco State University. From the book description: "Brings readers inside three North Carolina middle schools to show how students and teachers support and subvert the official curriculum through their questions, choices, viewpoints, and reactions. Most important, the book highlights how sex education's formal and informal lessons reflect and reinforce gender, race, and class inequalities. Ultimately critical of both conservative and liberal approaches, Fields argues for curricula that promote social and sexual justice. Sex education's aim need not be limited to reducing the risk of adolescent pregnancies, disease, and sexual activity. Rather, its lessons should help young people to recognize and contend with sexual desires, power, and inequalities."

Rigging the Game: How Inequality Is Reproduced in Everyday Life (Oxford University Press, 2007) by Michael Schwalbe, North Carolina State University. A brief, accessible introduction to the study of socioeconomic inequality in American society, using a "lively combination of incisive analysis and compelling fictional narratives" to show how inequalities of race, class, and gender are generated and perpetuated. The final chapter, "Escaping the Inequality Trap," shows "how inequality can be overcome." One college-professor reviewer writes of it: "I especially love the last chapter, with Schwalbe's hopeful conclusions and community-oriented approach. This is precisely what students need to learn to co-create the alternative institutions necessary to propel us forward into the emerging global multicultural millennium."

Such books nicely illustrate how sociology's sacred project is pursued and represented in sociological scholarship in different areas of research. With a little more discernment, we can perceive the influence of the same project in most other books produced by American sociology.

BOOKS REVIEWED IN *CONTEMPORARY SOCIOLOGY*

Still do not believe the book evidence? Let us look at the actual titles of books reviewed in the journal *Contemporary Sociology*, the ASA's official book-review periodical. This leading journal is tasked with publishing "reviews and critical discussions of recent works in sociology and related disciplines that merit the attention of sociologists." However, since not all sociological books can be reviewed, "a selection is made to reflect important trends and issues in the field."[2] We can therefore take *Contemporary Sociology* as covering a representative sample of the kind of books that mainstream sociology is producing and about which it considers worth knowing. Careful sampling of many issues is not necessary here, since the type and range of books in any given issue is similar to every other. One can pick any issue off the shelf at random and find essentially

2. http://www.asanet.org/journals/cs/cs.cfm.

the same thing, at least as relevant for my concern here. For present purposes, I examine the latest issue of that journal as of the time of this writing (May 2013). In it, we find a variety of different books reviewed, 60 in all, among which are the following titles (listed in the order they are reviewed in this issue):

- *The Making of Chicana/o Studies: In the Trenches of Academe*
- *Policing Pleasure: Sex Work, Policy, and the State in Global Perspective*
- *Equality with a Vengeance: Men's Rights Groups, Battered Women, and Antifeminist Backlash*
- *Patterns of Empire: The British and American Empires, 1688 to the Present*
- *Taking Liberties: The War on Terror and the Erosion of American Democracy*
- *Salaryman Masculinity: The Continuity and Change in the Hegemonic Masculinity in Japan*
- *Creating a New Racial Order: How Immigration, Multiracialism, Genomics, and the Young Can Remake Race in America*
- *Fire Management in the American West: Forest Politics and the Rise of Megafires*
- *The Crises of Multiculturalism: Racism in a Neoliberal Era*
- *Run to Failure: BP and the Making of the Deepwater Horizon Disaster*
- *One Nation under AARP: The Fight Over Medicare, Social Security, and America's Future*
- *Apartheid Vertigo: The Rise in Discrimination Against Africans in South Africa*
- *Coping with Social Change: Life Strategies of Workers in Poland's New Capitalism*
- *Good Jobs America: Making Work Better for Everyone*

- *Illicit Flirtations: Labor, Migration, and Sex Trafficking in Tokyo*
- *Motivational Dimensions of Social Movements and Contentious Collective Action*
- *They Say Cut Back, We Say Fight Back!: Welfare Activism in an Era of Retrenchment*
- *Prophetic Activism: Progressive Religious Justice Movements in Contemporary America*
- *How Economics Shapes Science*
- *The Collapse of American Criminal Justice*
- *Troubling Gender: Youth and Cumbia in Argentina's Music Scene*
- *A Match on Dry Grass: Community Organizing as a Catalyst for School Reform*
- *The Nuptial Deal: Same-Sex Marriage and Neo-Liberal Governance*
- *The Transformation of the American Pension System: Was it Beneficial for Workers?*
- *Globalization, Fear, and Insecurity: The Challenge for Cities North and South*
- *Prostitution, Harm, and Gender Inequality*
- *Follow the Leader: Politics isn't Just Childplay*
- *Greening the Media*
- *Intern Nation: How to Earn Nothing and Learn Little in the Brave New Economy*
- *Uncivil Rights: Teachers, Unions, and Race in the Battle for School Equity*
- *Bird on Fire: Lessons from the World's Least Sustainable City*
- *The Economics of Excess: Addiction, Indulgence, and Social Policy*

These titles represent more than one-half of the books reviewed in this issue. While one cannot always judge a book from its cover (title), my discussion above provides the right interpretive context for knowing what these books are about. Collectively, they are focused on threatening social problems (about which sociologists are the prophetic experts), injustices committed (about which sociologists are the whistle blowers), abuses by economically and politically (especially "neo-liberal") powerful elites (ditto on whistle blowing), and mobilizing social and political movements for sociopolitical and economic change (about which sociologists are the scientific experts and cheerleaders).

On the bad side, pleasures are policed, men are in backlash against feminists, America is an empire, the war on terror is eroding democracy, state policymakers are causing mega-forest fires, the neo-liberal era continues to be racist, BP has helped destroy the environment, Africans are discriminated against, capitalism in Poland is making workers' lives hard, welfare is being cut back, science is under the influence of economics, the American criminal justice system is collapsing, neo-liberal states cause trouble for same-sex marriages, prostitution causes harm and gender inequality, the media is not environmentally friendly, young interns are being exploited, schools are unequal, some cities are not sustainable, economic excess is addictive, and so on. On the good side, however, activist academics "in the trenches" have established Chicana/o studies, a combination of auspicious forces today are creating a New Racial Order in America, sociologists can tell how to make work better through good jobs, pro-welfare activists are fighting back against cuts, religion actually has at least one good thing to offer by sponsoring progressive justice movements, community organizers are working for school reform, and there still is a civil-rights battle for school equity. The bads outweigh the goods, but that is precisely why the world needs more sociology, to expose the bads and provide the correct vision and particular knowledge to overcome them.

Have I simply cherry-picked only the titles that validate my thesis? As a matter of fact, most of the books reviewed in this issue that bear titles less overtly manifesting American sociology's sacred project turn out in their actual content to manifest it clearly. Take, for example, the first book review in the table of contents not named above, *Sex Cells: The Medical Market for Eggs and Sperm*. At first glance, the title seems neutral and purely descriptive. On second glance, we realize that the title is a play on the adage that "sex sells," which introduces a nifty normative twist. Its argument, however, is not a critique of the immorality of artificial reproductive technologies or of selling body parts. It focuses rather, the review tells us, on gender inequality: "she [the book's author] found gender differences not only in pay, but in the framing of the donation." In the author's analysis, "the frame is a gendered stereotype of women as 'selfless, caring, and focused on relationships and family.'" This "gendered framing . . . is . . . a cultural reflection of modern maternal femininity and paternal masculinity."[3] The book is really about discrimination against women. I should say that this book sounds fascinating to me, well researched, and important. My point here is not that the book is bad—probably far from it. My point is simply that its lack of a title that is obviously oriented toward some activist, ideological, political theme does not mean it is disconnected from sociology's spiritual project.

Or take the immediately following book not listed above, the title of which is similarly relatively neutral: *Evidence-Based Healthcare in Context: Critical Social Science Perspectives*. One might never suspect by its title that this book has any tie to any sacred project,

---

3. Pp. 379–380. All references in the rest of this section are pages in *Contemporary Sociology*, May 2013, Vol. 42, No. 3 (not pages from the books reviewed).

yet a review of its content suggests otherwise. With evidence-based medicine (EBM), we learn, "standardization of knowledge is always fraught with political and social effects," including "three major unanticipated . . . problems with [its] implementation," which this book reveals. Included among them are a "privileging of knowledge," the fact that "biomedical research can be and is spun to support very different political and ideological positions," and that "some fear that EBM will reduce individual patients to a 'statistical patient,' where their personhood . . . and their preferences are lost." Thankfully, the research reveals, "instead of being applied directly, practitioners, patients, and others contextualize and resist these [EBM] guidelines."[4] Again, all of this sounds good, right, and believable to me. But we should not miss the relevant themes related to the larger sacred project: systemic oppression, problems of uniformity and privilege, the danger of support for the wrong political and ideological positions, threats to individual autonomy, and the need to "resist" the system. Irrelevant to sociology's sacred project this book is not—even if its connection is not as obvious and strong as many other books reviewed.

For a third and final example of the connection between even seemingly benign sociology books, their reviewers, and the spiritual project of American sociology, consider the third book reviewed in this issue of *Contemporary Sociology* that I did not list above, entitled *Moral Ambition: Mobilization and Social Outreach in Evangelical Megachurches*. On the face of it, this book seems to counter my thesis about sociology's secular sacred project, since it is precisely about more socially active evangelical Christians in the South who actually try to serve the poor and work toward racial reconciliation. In this, the reviewer observes, the book "problematizes many of the taken-for-granted assumptions about evangelicals, who are

4. Pp. 38–82.

often imagined as monolithic in their agreement and support for conservative Christian Right politics expressed in the public sphere on such topics as abortion and gay rights," and so "presents a more complicated picture of the [evangelical] experience than what we are usually presented through mainstream media representations."[5]

Nevertheless, between the book itself and the reviewer's presentation of it, American sociologists are generally confirmed in their standard stereotypical fears about and negative mental associations with evangelicalism. It works subtly here, however, and, I have no doubt, not particularly intentionally. How so? For general context, let us note that many American sociologists are worried about, if not frightened by, evangelical Christian "ambition" and "mobilization," and do not think very highly of evangelical megachurches, if they know anything about them at all—this I know from much experience as a scholar studying American evangelicalism. So this book's title contains three seemingly fairly benign words (ambition, mobilization, megachurches) that together and in the context of American evangelicalism raise red flags. To reinforce that, the review notes that, "chief among the issues that serve as historical and political backdrop to the story" are "the rise of evangelical Christians and the Christian Right during the 1980s and 1990s, with former President George W. Bush as a powerful symbol of that political as well as cultural ascendency."[6] Here, all of the standard mental and emotional associations are raised and reinforced, even if the ostensive point is to set up the subject of the book's study as different from Christian Right evangelicals. What becomes clear in the book and review, however, is that the socially progressive evangelicals that this study is about are a very small minority within these megachurches, who are stymied by the majority

5. Pp. 385–386.
6. P. 385.

of their evangelical co-religionists who do not agree with or support them. "One of the greatest challenges [one leader] faced was the lack of people [i.e., fellow evangelicals] to come out and actually do the work in a sustained manner. . . . His efforts were met with varying degrees of resistance from his peers." One effort to attempt to minister to people with HIV/AIDS, for example, "did not yield the result . . . anticipated," as it was "met with a condemnation of homosexuality rather than with compassion." Consequently, "those morally ambitious, socially engaged evangelicals take upon themselves a certain amount of risk both outside of their churches and inside them." Furthermore, half of their reason for wanting to care for the poor is to convert them to evangelical Christianity. Thus evangelical progressive social action is shown to be an instrumental method to accomplish religious proselytizing—definitely a bad thing. Moreover, this group of seemingly progressive evangelicals, the review suggests, needs to be understood in part as an expression of "compassionate conservatism . . . accompanying moves to reform [i.e., partly dismantle] the welfare state." In this way, their religious progressivism is actually exposed as at odds with "true" progressivism. Between these faults, many (white) evangelicals' inability to sacrifice time for the cause, "compassion fatigue," and the complications of race relations in the South, even these seemingly progressive evangelicals (not to mention their non-progressive fellow megachurch members) do not come out looking too good.

Thus, this book's "glimpse behind the veil of this segment of the conservative evangelical faith community" turns out to mostly reinforce the standard notions that American evangelicals really are a nearly uniform bloc of right-wing reactionaries, who make it difficult for, if not actually put at "risk," those few among them who attempt even the most timid acts of seemingly progressive social action.[7]

7. Pp. 385–386.

(Notice too that the language here ["glimpse behind the veil"] pre-supposes that American evangelicals, despite making up about 25 percent of the U.S. population,[8] are somehow an obscurely hidden "other," shrouded in mystery and secrecy—like the "veil" that like-wise covers the faces and hair of many orthodox Muslim women, who represent another kind of definite "other"—from the eyes of "ordinary" people [i.e., social scientists], who must therefore resort to a scholarly, glimpse-behind-the-veil voyeurism in order to possi-bly understand them in their exoticness.)

A relevant aside: Even the review's reference to the old "taken-for-granted assumptions about evangelicals, who are often imag-ined as monolithic in their agreement and support for conservative Christian Right politics" reveals a bizarrely stubborn-seeming de-termination among academics *never* to accept that these standard taken-for-granted assumptions are false. The fact is that decades of research have documented that the idea (myth) of "mono-lithic evangelicalism" is empirically false. Stephen Hart published a good book debunking this myth in 1992, I published a book in 2000 (with the very same publisher as the book under review here) showing the same thing in detail, Michael Hout and Andrew Gree-ley published a book making the identical point in 2006, and other scholars have also made clear the fact that American evangelicals are not a monolithic bloc that uniformly supports the Christian Right agenda.[9] *How many times must this simple fact be proven before*

8. According to 2012 data from the Pew Forum's Religion and Public Life Project, Reli-gious Landscape Survey: http://religions.pewforum.org/reports (accessed October 7, 2013).
9. Stephen Hart, 1992, *What Does the Lord Require?: How American Christians Think about Economic Justice*, New York: Oxford University Press; Christian Smith, 2000, *Chris-tian America?: What Evangelicals Really Want*, Berkeley: University of California Press; Andrew Greeley and Michael Hout, 2006, *The Truth About Conservative Christians: What They Think and What They Believe*, Chicago: University of Chicago Press; also see Nancy Ammerman, 1987, *Bible Believers*, New Brunswick: Rutgers University Press; Robert Robinson, 2009, "Two Approaches to Religion and Politics: Moral Cosmology

it is ever learned, believed, and remembered? Why is this new "insight" published in a sociological ethnography in 2011 taken to be a revelation? I do not fault the book's author, particularly, on this point, nor the reviewer; the problem is not them but the larger context in which they are working. Most revealing, in my view, is how this empirical fact can be treated among American sociologists in a top journal as if it were actually a surprise, something of which we have to take note. This reflects, I suggest, a determined passive-resistance on the part of sociologists to hear and believe the empirical fact that American evangelicals actually are a diverse group theologically, ideologically, and politically. But why? Because that fact is not easily assimilated into or comprehensible in light of American sociology's sacred project. It is a factual anomaly for the dominant paradigm and so treated as anomalies are: ignored. Sociologists far and wide thus proceed by default—to the extent that they focus on it at all—*as if* American evangelicalism is a monolithic bloc of right-wingers on the verge of imposing a theocracy, then ignore (if they are normal) or congratulate with relief (if they are enlightened) their peers who (recurrently) "find" that to be empirically untrue, but then proceed to forget that and suspect that evangelicalism is in fact a monolithic menace to be feared and opposed. Simply that many evangelical leaders seem clearly to be enemies of their sacred project is enough to justify the false stereotype about the entire population otherwise.

I could proceed here, book by book, to provide a more detailed analysis of how nearly every book reviewed in this particular issue of *Contemporary Sociology*—which provides just as representative a sample of American sociology books as any other issue—is actually more or less obviously or indirectly reflective of the sacred

and Subcultural Identity," *Journal for the Scientific Study of Religion*, 48: 650–669; Robert Robinson and Nancy Davis, 1996, "Religious Orthodoxy in American Society: The Myth of a Monolithic Camp," *Journal for the Scientific Study of Religion*, 35: 229–245.

project of American sociology. But to continue analyzing book by book would grow tedious. I hope I have said enough to suggest the plausibility of my argument. To be clear, again, I am not criticizing sociology book authors or book reviewers or book publishers or *Contemporary Sociology* or its fine editor, per se. Their work is, for present purposes, merely indicative. It simply offers one more piece of evidence that fits together with the whole into a larger picture that illuminates and validates my case that American sociology is not merely a "science of society," but is and has a spiritual project that defines and governs its professional assumptions, interests, and practices—even down to the nitty-gritty level of ordinary book reviews.

American Sociological Review Articles

Enough said about books. Let us shift to what appear to be the more scientific publications of sociology: journal articles. And let us go all the way to the top, to examine articles published in what is commonly regarded as American sociology's best journal, the *American Sociological Review* (*ASR*). Like *Contemporary Sociology*, the *ASR* is officially sponsored and published by the ASA as its flagship journal, and is one of the two holy grails of journal publishing, along with the *American Journal of Sociology*. If any sociological journal could be immune to the kind of sacred project I am describing here, it would be *ASR*. But is it actually? Rarely does one find in *ASR* the kind of title or argument we have seen in sociology books. The journal's image and style of scientist rigor forbid it. Here, if nowhere else, sociology has to prove that it is just as serious a science as, say, physics. So, one generally does not find articles in *ASR* with titles like, "We Say Fight Back!"

Yet a sensitized examination below the surface of appearances reveals that even the *ASR* belongs to and advances sociology's sacred project. It plays a particular role in scientifically legitimating that project, but it in no way transcends or contradicts it. How so? In order not to drag readers through an analysis of gobs of sampled articles compiled from many issues, I will again examine one issue of the journal, selected randomly among all recent issues. The method by which I sample is to commit to analyzing the next issue to come in the mail after my writing this very paragraph, before I have even looked at it and regardless of what it happens to contain. That should again help to rebuff suspicions of cherry-picking.

(Two weeks later.) Okay, so, I have now received and studied the pre-determinedly sampled issue of *ASR* and examined its contents.[10] What do I find? What follows is a brief descriptive analysis of each article in this issue in the order they are published.

"Social Isolation in America: An Artifact."[11] This methodological piece focuses on the apparent shrinking of interpersonal social networks among Americans over recent decades, arguing that the measured shrinkage in number of close social ties does not reflect actual change in the size of people's social networks, but instead is a methodological artifact of particularly poor training and fatigue of survey interviewers, who as a result generate fewer names of respondents' close ties. This suggests that recent works that have raised alarms about the (alleged) loss of "social capital" in America, an increase in social isolation, and a decline in social connectivity among Americans are based on errors. On the surface, this technical methodological article appears to have no connection to American sociology's sacred project. In fact, however, it does, as follows.

Scholars and journalists who have raised concerns about declining social capital and loss of social support resulting from the shrinkage of social ties and relational connectivity tend in so doing

10. June 2013, Vol. 78, No. 3.
11. By Anthony Paik and Kenneth Sanchagrin, pp. 339–360.

to critique implicitly or explicitly the direction that American culture and society have taken in recent decades.[12] A common worry is that changes since the early 1960s—such as an increase in women working, the breakdown of stable nuclear families, the increasing penetration of society by television and new digital media and technology, expansion of the welfare state, greater independence among youth, and the loss of a shared cultural language of community and responsibility—are leading to gradual breakdown of and dysfunction in society. Concerns over moral and social breakdown, chaos, and disintegration are also historically associated—though not always accurately so—with "conservatives." And the sociocultural changes just mentioned are many of the same changes that the spiritual project of American society positively advocates or at least tolerates. So, if Americans' interpersonal social networks actually are shrinking over time, and thus social capital, social support, and community relations are eroding, then sociology's sacred project is implicated in sociocultural changes that can be criticized for being socially destructive. This article, however, claims that those concerns are groundless, that Americans' social networks are not really shrinking. Therefore, all of the sociocultural changes since the 1960s that critics have associated with the decline of social capital, connectivity, and community are not in fact really problems at all. So they can continue changing America in ways that sociology's sacred project supports without any harm to society.[13]

12. For examples, Robert Putnam, 2001, *Bowling Alone: The Collapse and Revival of American Community*, New York: Touchstone; Robert Bellah et al., 1985, *Habits of the Heart: Individualism and Commitment in American Life*, Berkeley: University of California Press; James D. Hunter, 2000, *Death Of Character Moral Education In An Age Without Good Or Evil*, Basic Books; Andres Duany, Elizabeth Plater-Zyberk, Jeff Speck, 2010, *Suburban Nation: The Rise of Sprawl and the Decline of the American Dream*, New York: North Point Press.

13. Also see Claude Fischer's fascinating work that relates to these issues: 2011, *Still Connected: Family and Friends in America since 1970*, New York: Russell Sage Foundation.

(To be clear, I am not saying that the authors were consciously aware of or directly motivated by this logic to write this article. They were no doubt primarily concerned with the methodological issues involved in measuring social ties well and their implications for arguments about declining social capital and community. Nonetheless, the article does frame its own significance in some of the terms I just explained, and—whatever the authors' conscious interests and motivations—the larger implication of the conclusion of the article in sociology's universe is exactly what I just described.)

"The Capitalist Machine: Computerization, Workers' Power, and the Decline in Labor's Share within U.S. Industries."[14] This article demonstrates that the declining share of U.S. national income suffered by working labor has come at the expense of the rising share of capitalists' income, and that the main factor causing the loss in labor's share of income was the erosion of workers' "positional power," partly as an outcome of "class-biased technological change"—that is, the computerization of work that favored employers over workers. At the heart of growing inequality stand structures of power relations organizing social classes, not neutral market mechanisms and outcomes related to increase productivity of skilled workers, as many economists would have it. With findings supported by a unique dataset, the author concludes that "capitalists' profits play a crucial role in the process of social stratification," "capitalists have grabbed the lion's share of income growth over the past three decades," and "it is clearly capitalists who have rarely had it so good."

The connection here to sociology's sacred project is clear. Socioeconomic equality is an end goal toward which to work. The fact that inequality has been increasing instead is a social problem caused by differentials in power between social classes. The author

---

14. Tali Kristal, pp. 361–389, quotes are from pp. 361 and 383.

offers no statements about how to reverse growing income inequality, but the mere analysis and conclusion themselves make clear that an identifiable social problem exists, that the rich and powerful are responsible for it, and what is needed to combat it.

"The Care Economy? Gender, Economic Restructuring, and Job Polarization in the U.S. Labor Market."[15] This article argues that the polarization of the American job structure at the end of the twentieth century (growth in the best and worst jobs, but not much growth in the middle) is significantly explained by the rise of "care work" in the economy—that is, jobs involving care for other people engaged in tasks that used to be served by family and kin, and typically performed by women. Such jobs expanded dramatically in the United States after 1983, are often among the lowest-paying, are often worked by women and minorities, and so contributed significantly to a restructuring of American jobs associated with general wage inequality and gender and racial economic inequality. Wages in care work have also been suppressed by cost-cutting efforts in the public sector, little labor market power of care workers, gender discrimination, and intentional efforts by owners in this sector. Thus, "care work is implicated in growing and persistent class inequalities as well as the evolution of gender inequalities." These "findings highlight the importance of inequality among women and the ways economic restructuring has benefited college-educated women far more than low-skilled women."

Furthermore, "if the care economy continues on its current trajectory, its dynamics may increasingly affect wage inequality dynamics. In particular, to the extent that care is undercompensated due to its characterization as a public good, care work wage growth may be suppressed. Collective action of care workers themselves will also be important." The author sees "professionalization

---

15. Rachel Dwyer, pp. 390–416, quotes are from pp. 411, 412.

and unionization" of this sector as holding the potential to improve wages. In any case, the growth of care work "raises important questions about the future of the U.S. economy" and thus economic inequalities. Longer-term outcomes will "depend on institutional shifts, as more states and the federal government get involved in early childhood care. Dilemmas in funding and organizing care will likely only become more pressing as our population ages and generational divides increasingly coincide with class and race differences." The author concludes that "economic growth and the kind of job opportunities available in the U.S. economy will increasingly be affected by political and institutional debates over the quality and provision of care, and by the way that caring labor evolves between the workers and organizations that increasingly provide care and the individuals and families who need it."

Again, the scientific contribution to the pursuit of sociology's sacred project is clear here. The sources of economic, wage, gender, and racial inequality, polarization, and discrimination are revealed; and suggestions for ways to reduce inequality—collective action, professionalization, unionization, and the right outcomes of political and institutional debates—are recommended. Sociology is thus put to use to draw attention to the social problem of care work–based growing economic inequality in the U.S. economy and to suggest means to transform it.

"The Corner and the Crew: The Influence of Geography and Social Networks on Gang Violence."[16] This article neither uncovers a new social problem to generate concern about nor takes an explicit normative position on gangs. The purpose of the article is to demonstrate that urban street gang violence is shaped both by geography (proximity of gang turf and prior conflict between gangs)

---

16. Andrew Papachristos, David Hureau, and Anthony Braga, pp. 417–447, quote on p. 438.

and social networks (reciprocity and status seeking). Findings show that both spatial and network processes mediate racial effects on gang violence, indicating the primacy of place and social group. The article describes the extent of gang violence in the United States as "striking," but gang violence is not new news and the value added here is not about the social problem of gang violence. Rather, the article's contribution concerns the ways that "geography and social networks intersect and intertwine to produce" gang violence. This strictly methodological concern means the only link of this article to sociology's sacred project is its demonstrating the social scientific contribution that sociology can make to better understanding social problems, like urban gang violence, and then presumably through informed policy measures to help combat them.

"Gender and Twenty-First-Century Corporate Crime: Female Involvement and the Gender Gap in Enron-Era Corporate Frauds."[17] This article examines gender differences in recent corporate financial scandals, showing that women were much less likely than men to have been involved in corporate crime between 2002 and 2009 that involved major indictments. Female conspirators were not only less often involved in corporate financial scandals, but played more minor roles in the crimes than men, profited financially less than men from them (even when statistically controlling for corporate rank and magnitude of the role played in the crime), and were more reactive than proactive in their decision to participate. Women tended not to cook up the illegal schemes themselves, but were drawn in by men with whom they had strong relationships or because they occupied key positions in accounting or compliance and so were necessary players to recruit into the crimes. Motivating the study in part is the fact that such "fraudulent schemes

17. Darrell Steffensmeier, Jennifer Schwartz, and Michael Roche, pp. 448–476, quotes are on pp. 448, 449, 469, 470, 471.

and corporate corruption scandals played key roles in the onset and in determining the severity of the past three economic recessions in the United States" (1990, 2001, and 2007). The study thus follows a tradition in sociology of interest in white-collar crime, spurred by one scholar's "revulsion with elites whose financial manipulations caused the 1929 stock market crash and the 1930s Depression." This article's focus on gender differences in financial scandals, however, is meant to "contribute particularly to the broad and rising interest across sociology in gender stratification" (inequality).

One theoretical observation of the article is that the same forces that exclude women from positions of corporate power generally also limit their participation in corporate crime: "exclusionary practices that limit women's entry into some roles in the economy" make it such that "women are likely either excluded entirely from lucrative criminal conspiracies or are utilized in sex-typed ways deemed most effective for the enterprise." In short, job discrimination against women is matched by discrimination against women in their ability to commit white-collar crimes, meaning that "minimal changes have occurred in at least some fundamental forms of gender stratification." Moreover, "a fundamental irony" of this gender discrimination is that many females were especially vulnerable to being criminally indicted because their midlevel positions "made them a useful tool for the prosecution to gain evidence and to turn state's witness against co-conspirators." So not only are women left out of the lucrative illegalities, but, when caught, they are also especially targeted in criminal investigations.

Finally, the article raises this pragmatic question about reducing corporate financial crimes: "Would more women in positions of corporate leadership and power reduce corporate fraud? There are good reasons for believing so." Women, it is suggested, might act more ethically than men, be more careful in taking financial risks, and be less likely to cultivate a "criminogenic organizational culture." Those are mere hypotheses, however, so "testing these alternative hypotheses awaits growth in the number of women in corporate leadership positions." Not only is achieving equality in job opportunity for women a matter of principle, the reader can infer, but it would likely reduce corporate crime and thus decrease the chances and severity of national economic recessions.

In more than most of the other articles in this issue, the influence of American sociology's spiritual project is evident in its focus on unmasking gender exclusion, inequalities, and exploitation in the workplace, in showing that men are the real bad guys when it comes to corporate crime, in the framing of corporate fraud as a major cause of economic recessions, and in the normative suggestion that equalizing women's positions in corporate leadership and power would likely help to solve such social problems. In brief, the article's concentration on gender exclusion and inequality, elite corporate misconduct causing recession, male instrumental utilization of women, and the possible moral superiority of women and social need for their corporate upward mobility make this article a beautiful expression of sociology's sacred project through (what strikes me as) impressive and fascinating social scientific scholarship.

"Does Specialization Explain Marriage Penalties and Premiums?"[18] This article seeks to better understand "the distribution of marriage's costs and benefits by gender and parental status." Specifically, it attempts to explain why married men tend to earn higher incomes than unmarried men, and fathers higher income than nonfathers. The particular theoretical explanation it tests is the "specialization hypothesis," that men can devote more effort to earning wages when they have wives to assume more responsibilities for

18. Alexandra Killewald and Margaret Gough, pp. 477–502, quotes are from pp. 477, 478, 496.

household work. If this hypothesis explained the "marriage premium," then wives' earnings should go down as their husbands' go up. The empirical findings, however, show that both men's and women's wages increase with marriage through similar processes, although men benefit more than women from marriage. However, men's wages increase as they become fathers, whereas women becoming mothers pay a penalty in earnings—"parenting premiums" go only to men, in other words.

Theoretically, the hypothesis of specialization within households is not validated by the findings, therefore, since women also benefit from marriage, albeit less so than men. Other mechanisms must explain how marriage increases wages for the married, including, possibly, discrimination by employers in favor of married people, on the presumption that the married are more reliable workers. Empirically, the article shows that both sexes benefit in earnings from marriage, although men benefit significantly more than women; and that men especially benefit from becoming fathers.

The substantive concern here that engages and advances sociology's sacred project is its focus on measuring and explaining gender differences in wages that are associated with marriage (which is conceptualized as a penalizing or advantaging social institution) and with parenting, in both of which men tend to be the bigger winners than women. Unstated but also obvious in the analysis is the fact that unmarried men and women lose in the wage game to those who are married, for reasons that are not entirely clear or perhaps just.

"The Shadow of Indebtedness: Bridewealth and Norms Constraining Female Reproductive Autonomy."[19] This final article

---

19. Christine Horne, F. Nii-Amoo Dodoo, and Naa Dodua Dodoo, pp. 503–520, quotes are from pp. 503, 517, 518.

in this issue examines the role that "bridewealth" plays in constraining the autonomy of women in Ghana. Bridewealth consists of payment from the man's family to the woman's family in the form of "livestock, clothes, fabric, beads, household goods, imported products, drinks, and money," as a necessary part of the marriage bargain (conceived here as an "exchange structure"). The article opens thus: "Women in Africa have constricted reproductive autonomy. Their reproductive and sexual behaviors are a product not only of their own desires, but more so of normative constraints imposed by family and community members. Women's lack of control over their reproductive behavior has a range of [negative] health implications. . . . Because marriage in Africa occurs early and is virtually universal, understanding the factors that constrain the autonomy of married women is particularly important." The article finds that bridewealth indeed "strengthens normative constraints on women's reproductive autonomy. . . . [It] institutionalizes patterns of obligation that require women to defer to their male partners in the reproductive domain." The article concludes with this policy recommendation: "Efforts to improve the lives of African women must take into account existing marriage practices and related gender norms. Policies that fail to factor in the normative obligations created by bridewealth payments may have limited success." Here, "improving the lives of African women" is equated, as a good western feminist presupposition, with expanding "women's reproductive autonomy."

Nobody could build a convincing case about American sociology having and being a sacred project using *ASR* articles alone; the publication is simply too scientist for that to happen. Yet, in the context of the larger body of evidence presented in this book, what we find in *ASR* does fit my sacred-project thesis well. In various ways, the subject matter of the articles, the ways that their concerns and concepts are framed, and some of the key terminology in them clearly reflect the sacred project I described above. In one case, a concern with personal "autonomy" and self-determination of women's reproductive experience is central, and people's lives are said to be "improved" as constraints on their autonomy are removed. In more than half of the articles, exposing and understanding gender inequalities in marriage and the workplace play central roles. In all but two of the articles, elites, capitalists, employers, corporate leaders, powerful upper classes, class-biased technologies, and (in the case of implicitly "backward" Africa) powerful family members and kin exert pernicious influences on individuals' lives. Solutions to problems consist not only of expanded women's autonomy but also collective-action protests, unionization, professionalization of low-status occupations, and more methodological sophistication in sociological research. Furthermore, the alleged social changes that sociology's spiritual project mostly applauds are—contrary to the worries of "communitarians" and "conservatives"—shown to be in fact not damaging social capital, community, or connectedness, so we can be confident to let them proceed apace without any negative social consequences. Countering the sacred project's default view of (heterosexual) marriage as being suspect as an oppressive and exploitative institution, one article in this issue showed that marriage actually enhances people's lives, in the form of higher wages—but not unlikely in part because of employee discrimination against unmarried people—and even then men benefit significantly more than women. Only one article in this issue—that on urban street gang violence—was not obviously directly tied to American sociology's sacred project, beyond simply being about how social science can help to understand and solve the social problem of gang violence. Otherwise, the raft of articles in this issue tilted clearly in the supportive direction of the sacred project to which, explicitly or implicitly, subtly or obviously, the *ASR*, the ASA, and American sociology as a whole are committed.[20]

Let me remind readers that, simply because I am pointing out this evidence for sociology being a particular sacred project, this does not mean I am making fun of these published articles, questioning their quality and value, denigrating the general moral commitments that lay behind them, or otherwise opposing or dismissing such scholarship. Even though I find the writing style of most of these articles to be atrociously boring, I do find the substance of their investigations to be fascinating and important, their (usually implicit) moral concerns valid, and the scholarly analyses in them to be impressive. I am also persuaded that what they are claiming to be true is (aside from some of the normative framing) indeed factually true. And, as I explain below, while I am committed to a different spiritual project than the one that dominates American sociology, I find much overlap on specific concerns between the two, and so I recurrently find myself in genuine sympathy with and supportive of many (but not all) of the concerns of sociology's sacred project. I do believe that what is good in sociology's sacred project can be reframed in a much

20. Incidentally, among the handful of books advertised in a two-page spread at the back of the journal (pp. 522–523) is one (*Beauty Pays: Why Attractive People are More Successful*) demonstrating how beautiful people are advantaged and more successful than less-attractive people, who are discriminated against; another (*The Imperative of Integration*) explains why affirmative action is a necessary tool to achieve full racial integration in order to eliminate disparities across races in life outcomes; and a third (*Waiting for José: The Minutemen's Pursuit of America*) gives us an inside view of the "Minutemen" who patrol the U.S./Mexican border for illegal immigrants, as men driven not so much by political and ideological convictions but by a lost sense of personal meaning, purpose, and identity. In addition, most of the six books advertised on the back cover of this issue similarly embody and reflect the concerns of sociology's spiritual project, ranging from exposés of how economic disadvantage leads to youth crime and violence and how the persistence of racial segregation in American housing leads to neighborhood violence, to a challenge to the supposed superiority (advocated by "experts") of "natural" breast-feeding by mothers (compared to the more typical practice among working-women of formula bottle feeding), and a celebration of enlightened (i.e., influenced by feminism) "superdads" who properly balance work and family.

more valid and realistic philosophical anthropology, philosophy of science, and moral philosophy. But even as that project stands, I can and do affirm very many specific points in it—something worth keeping in mind during my analysis. My investigation here should not be interpreted as the hostile opposition of a conservative (gasp!), which I am not. Nor should my poking fun at colleagues and my own discipline and profession be taken as pure antagonistic derision. The reality is much more complicated than that.

ASA NATIONAL MEETING THEMES

The ASA has organized a number of "activist" conference programs for its national meetings. These include the following official program themes, chosen by each year's elected ASA President: "Real Utopias: Emancipatory Projects, Institutional Designs, and Possible Futures" (2012), "Toward a Sociology of Citizenship: Inclusion, Participation, and Rights" (2010), "Discourses of Stability and Change" (2009), "Is Another World Possible?" (2007), "Great Divides: Transgressing Boundaries" (2006), "Public Sociologies" (2004), "Oppression, Domination & Liberation: Challenges for the 21st Century" (2000), "Inequality and Social Policy" (1998), and "Social Change: Opportunities and Constraints" (1996). The program theme for the 2013 ASA conference, which meets a few months from when I am writing this, is "Interrogating Inequalities: Linking Micro and Macro." The ASA President's explanation of this theme begins by nothing that "Sociologists want more than just to chart patterns of social inequalities. [We want to ask:] How is inequality made and, therefore, *could potentially be unmade*?"[21] The "theme statement"

---

21. From the cover page of the Annual Meeting information and program summary included in the June 2013 issue of *Footnotes* (italics added for emphasis).

for 2013 on the ASA website says that "No set of questions is more fundamental to sociology than those about inequality—what is it, why is it, how does it come about, and *what can we do to change it?* . . . Through what processes does this work? *How can we intervene in those processes?* . . . Our task at these meetings is to locate the key junctures among these multilevel processes that *provide the levers by which* different sorts of inequalities among people and groups are systematically made or *unmade* in the contemporary context. This is the essential first *step towards changing those inequalities*."[22] There it is in black and white, straight from the ASA President: Sociology's central goal is to eliminate social inequalities.

Showing that this outlook is not anomalous, the ASA 2014 national meeting's program theme was announced as the very similar topic, "Hard Times: The Impact of Economic Inequality on Families and Individuals." The President's thematic description of it is this:

> America is a land of inequality. Moreover, the scope of economic inequality has grown sharply in recent decades. . . . The program will highlight social science research documenting the breadth and depth of economic inequality and the consequences for virtually every sphere of social life. . . . The program will examine variations in economic inequality by race and ethnicity, gender, and immigrant status. . . . In addition to examining the poor and middle-class, special attention will also be paid to the experiences of the very wealthy. . . . . The focus on "Hard Times" . . . *will critically examine programs of change, whether in the form of social movements or policy interventions.* . . . Please plan to join us in San Francisco in 2014.[23]

---

22. http://www.asanet.org/AM2013/meeting_theme.cfm (italics added for emphasis).
23. http://www.asanet.org/am2014/Theme.cfm, accessed October 14, 2013 (italics added for emphasis).

Among its own, at least, the ASA is explicit that American sociology is not only about conducting and sharing scientific scholarship, but also *promoting social-change activism through social movements and policy interventions designed to eliminate socioeconomic inequalities.* That activist project—which I am saying is ultimately a Durkheimian sacred—and the particular view of human persons that underwrites it stand at the heart of American sociology as a discipline.

ASA SECTIONS

American sociology's sacredly driven activity is organized into "sections" at a national level through the ASA, according to members' general areas of interest/activism. The ASA's total membership of more than 14,000 is divided into 52 different sections by interest areas. New sections may be formed by members, but organizers must first recruit at least 100 members to become a Section-in-Formation, and then 300 within two years to continue as an official ASA section. Sections are allotted sessions at national meetings in proportion to their membership size, in which they are allowed to organize panels for paper presentations, author-meets-critics panels, business meetings, and so on. Some sections are enormous, others are smaller. In what follows, I list the ASA sections by size (with section membership numbers in parentheses[24]), grouped into three categories: (1) those that most obviously serve and promote sociology's sacred project, (2) those that do not obviously on the face of it serve that project, but which much of the activity within actually does, and (3) those that seem not particularly connected to sociology's sacred project.

24. These numbers were provided to me by the ASA's membership administrator in 2013, and, while they obviously change somewhat over time, are fairly stable in the short run.

ASA Sections at the Vanguard of Sociology's Sacred Project

Sex and Gender (1,083)	Race, Gender, and Class (901)
Political Sociology (835)	Collective Behavior & Social Movements (779)
Sociology of Education (760)	Racial & Ethnic Minorities (773)
Family (731)	Inequality, Poverty & Mobility (678)
Global/Transnational Sociology (651)	International Migration (621)
Science, Knowledge, & Technology (496)	Sociology of Sexualities (485)
Environment & Technology (467)	Sociology of Development (404)
Sociology of Mental Health (402)	Labor and Labor Movements (393)
Political Economy of the World-System (382)	Latino/a Sociology (330)
Sociological Practice & Public Sociology (311)	Marxist Sociology (288)
Consumers and Consumption (261)	Body and Embodiment (259)
Peace, War, & Social Conflict (252)	Human Rights (246)
Disability and Society (191)	Alcohol, Drugs and Tobacco (170)

Together, these 26 sections comprise 13,149 sociologist members (although not uniquely so, since many sociologists belong to more than one section). The vast majority of the members in these sections are engaged in research, publication, and teaching that actively promote the spiritual project of American sociology, in ways that are fairly obvious. They struggle for the elimination of inequalities based on gender, sexualities, race, ethnicity, social class, and bodily differences. They expose the hidden oppressions and abuses involved in science, technology, family life, international migration regimes, social control of the body, globalization, disability, capitalist consumerism, mental health treatment systems, chemical addictions, abuse of the environment, and the neo-liberal global economy. They study (and often valorize and promote) social movements, collective protest action, labor movements, public-school reforms, and "public sociology." Some sections are explicitly Marxist and interested in neo-Marxist world-systems theory. Others employ standard categorizations organizing feminists and scholars in GLBTQ and queer studies. Eight of the top 12 sections have directly to do with sex, gender, intimate relationships, race, class, ethnicity, poverty, and power—the core substantive concerns of sociology's sacred project.

Next consider 22 other ASA sections, which, simply by reading their names, one might not guess their members to be engaged in the sacred project described above. Yet a greater familiarity with what many of these sections' members are doing in research, publishing, and teaching reveals that many of them, too, are devotees to sociology's spiritual project (remember too that many are also no doubt members in the sections above).

ASA Sections Less Obviously but in Many Ways Still Promoting Sociology's Sacred Project

Sociology of Culture (1,112)

Organizations, Occupation and Work (929)

Economic Sociology (782)

Medical Sociology (978)

Theory (779)

Comparative-Historical Sociology (728)

Teaching and Learning (713)	Social Psychology (637)
Sociology of Religion (595)	Community & Urban Sociology (587)
Aging and the Life Course (549)	Crime, Law, & Deviance (553)
Sociology of Population (456)	Methodology (389)
Sociology of Law (372)	Children & Youth (357)
Asia/Asian America (318)	Communication and Information (292)
Altruism, Morality and Social Solidarity (255)	Sociology of Emotions (253)
Evolution, Biology & Society (154)	Animals and Society (147)

What does it mean to promote the sacred project of American sociology through scholarship and teaching related to these section areas? Sociologists demonstrate, for example, how unjust, exploitative, and oppressive many jobs are in the American economy, or how little intergenerational occupational mobility there is in the United States (Organizations, Occupation and Work). Others study the long historical struggles of various movements and revolutions to achieve the limited (but inadequate) democracy and freedoms enjoyed by modern people (Comparative-Historical Sociology). Yet others investigate how to promote family planning and population control (Sociology of Population). Still others study racial and economic segregation in urban settings (Community & Urban Sociology). And so on. Not all or necessarily even most sociologists who are members of these sections are fighting at the vanguard of sociology's sacred project. But I would venture to say—based on three decades of personal observation, relationships with sociologists, and ongoing examinations of the articles and books these scholars produce—that the majority of work published (and very likely teaching offered) by sociologists in these sections ultimately feeds into support for and the promotion of the spiritual project. I cannot conduct a systematic investigation to "prove" that, but I am confident that one well conducted would validate my claim (as my analysis of books and articles above suggests).

Finally, four ASA sections—representing only 679 members, a mere 5.2 percent of the size of the first group of sections above—seem to have little to do topically with the sacred project of American sociology that I have described. Their members may very well be devoted disciples of that project, but nothing in the section names or known activities—which mostly have to do with methodology and disciplinary history—suggests an interest in sociology's sacred vision and mission.

ASA Sections Seemingly Not Related to Sociology's Sacred Project

History of Sociology (190)	Mathematical Sociology (202)
Rationality and Society (145)	Ethnomethodology and Conversation Analysis (142)

In addition to studying the ASA sections that do exist, it is also worth considering the *potential* ASA sections that do *not* exist, and why they do not. For example, in principle, there is no reason why sociologists committed to different kind of sacred projects could not as sociologists legitimately be interested in topics that would give rise to the following kinds of possible association sections:

- Human Virtues & Flourishing
- Meditation, Transcendent Consciousness, Society
- Augustinian/Thomistic Sociology

- Efficient Economic Growth
- Meritocratic Inequalities & Just Deserts
- Human–Divine Intersections/Transgressions
- Pain/Suffering/Personal Growth
- Protecting Life from Conception to Natural Death
- Global Religious Persecution & Martyrdom
- Samsara & Illusions of Individuality in Society
- Sin/Evil/Human Corruption
- Mysteries, Miracles, Ineffability, Social Order
- Gender Complementarities
- Modernity & Spiritual Retardation

Those hypothetical sections are unimaginable, laughable, of course, in the context of American sociology. That is because American sociologists are an extremely particular group of people, most of whom are more or less committed to a very distinct sacred project, which much of the world, even much of the population of America, does not share. Of course, it might actually take a sociological perspective to see this, but, in fact, billions of other not-idiotic people (potential sociologists) from different cultures, religions, and worldviews, might find any of the above section topics of great interest and importance. Certain of these imagined non-sections at least are no more idiosyncratic than some of the smaller ASA sections now in existence. I realize that some if not many American sociologists might say that any "sociologist" who would be interested in being part of any of those sections is clearly "not a real sociologist." And that is precisely the sort of thing that our anthropologist sisters and brothers call "closed-minded ethnocentrism" and many sociologists criticize for "essentializing" mere social constructions.

Examining ASA section names does little in and of itself to verify my claim about the existence and influence of American sociology's sacred project, a sacred cause in the Durkheimian sense. But as part

THE SACRED PROJECT OF AMERICAN SOCIOLOGY

of the larger body of evidence that I am presenting here, it makes a contribution. A look at ASA's organized sections—especially by those quite familiar with American sociology and sociologists— does reveal the kinds of interests and concerns of most American sociologists. And those do comport well with my account of that spiritual project.

A TEXTBOOK CASE

Each academic semester, tens of thousands of college students in the United States take "Introduction to Sociology" classes, usu- ally as core requirements of their programs for graduation. In most cases, they are assigned introductory textbooks as required reading. What are those textbooks teaching students? I analyzed the three most popular introduction sociology textbooks to see whether American sociology's sacred project is present in them. I found that it is indeed a central part of their (not very) "hidden curriculum."[25] In fact, because sociology's sacred project is ubiqui- tously expressed in so many ways in these textbooks, I will only be

---

25. Three sociology texts appear on the spring 2012 Amazon.com list of 100 bestselling textbooks in all disciplines (https://images-na.ssl-images-amazon.com/images/G/01/ rainier/help/US_Top100_Textbooks_Spring2012.html): (ranked 14th of 100) *So- ciety: The Basics* (11th ed.) by John J. Macionis, (ranked 16th) *Essentials of Sociology, A Down-to-Earth Approach* (9th ed.) by James M. Henslin; (ranked 81st) *Sociology: A Brief Introduction* (9th ed.) by Richard T. Schaefer. In her 2011 study of most popular Introduction to Sociology textbooks ("What Sociology Teaches Us about Gender: The Underlying Messages within Introduction to Sociology Textbooks," MA thesis, San Diego State University, Spring 2011), Jessica White's search found the following five (in order of sales) as sociology's bestselling textbooks, the top three of which match my list exactly: *Society: The Basics* (10th ed., 2008) by John Macionis, *Essentials of Sociol- ogy: A Down-to-Earth Approach* (8th ed., 2008) by James Henslin, *Sociology: A Brief Introduction* (8th ed., 2008) by Richard Schaefer, *The Real World: An Introduction to Sociology* (2nd ed., 2009) by Kerry Ferris and Jill Stein, and *You May Ask Yourself: An Introduction to Thinking like a Sociologist* (1st ed., 2008) by Dalton Conley.

able, given space constraints here, to document a small piece of it all (with, I am afraid, less restraint in my tone of antipathy than in the rest of this book, though for good reasons, I hope the reader sees). I proceed by focusing on the best-selling Introduction to Sociology textbook, John Macionis' *Society: The Basics*.[26] Reading through it, page by page, sociology's sacred, spiritual project shines through like a beacon. At times, in fact, the textbook reads like a training manual for spiritual novices.

The textbook literally begins immediately on page 2 (page 1 is a photo) by highlighting the (then) fact of legal discrimination against same-sex marriage in the United States. The very first block of text beneath the "chapter overview" points out, while discussing why people marry whom they marry, that "Society has many 'rules' about whom we should and should not marry. In all states but Massachusetts, Vermont, New Hampshire, Connecticut, and Iowa, along with the District of Columbia, the law rules out half the population, banning people from marrying someone of the same sex, even if the couple is deeply in love."[27] That, apparently, is the most important place to begin an "introduction" to "the basics" of "society."

Next, in the very first sentence of the main text, the textbook calls into question the traditional idea of human "free will" by asserting that "Our decisions do not simply result from what philosophers call 'free will.' Sociology teaches us that our social world guides our life choices in much the same way that the seasons influence our choice of clothing." Alas, American sociology here

---

26. 11th edition (2011)—not that new or old editions change much, since the introducing of "new" is primarily a way to forcibly make obsolete the innumerable used textbooks assigned in previous semesters, so that current students are forced to buy the latest edition at full price; in short, issuing new editions is mostly about increasing profits, not educational value (that is, exploitation).

27. All quotes from this textbook in the pages that follow here come from pp. 2–33 of Macionis, presented in order of these pages in the textbook.

immediately demonstrates its common philosophical ineptitude, since (apart from the fact that no serious thinker would actually say that humans act completely with "free will"), acting with free will to choose one's clothing and having one's choices of clothing shaped by seasonal conditions are obviously perfectly compatible. With that, the reader is then told that "Sociology is the systematic study of human society."

What is obvious to the alert reader—but probably less so to most undergraduate student readers—here and throughout is how consistently the text frames what matters about "society" and what a "systematic study" of society should focus upon and why. Starting immediately and continuing throughout the text's 500+ pages is a unrelenting focus on social problems that demand redress for the sake of justice and equality—particularly discrimination against women, racism, social class unfairness, income inequality, women's lack of reproductive choice, structural unemployment, the social exclusion of gays, problems with economic globalization, male privilege, misunderstanding of minorities, prejudice against slum residents, and gender double standards. In relation to these social problems, however, readers are told that "Sociology has helped shape public policy . . . in countless ways, from radical desegregation and school busing to laws regulating divorce." Sociology thus comes off as the science of social problem solving. The author then blithely cites in the text a discredited 1985 study on unequal economic outcomes of divorce for men and women—the very one that, as I explain in the next section, contained grossly exaggerated statistics resulting from (eventually) admitted mistakes in the research, which were uncovered and refuted *15 years before this textbook edition was published*, as if no problems existed with that flawed study.

In the next section, on "Sociology and Personal Growth," the text again (second time in five pages) questions the idea of free human choice, personal responsibility, and ordinary views of life, writing that sociology "helps us assess the truth of 'common sense.' We all take many things for granted, but that does not make them true. One good example is the idea that we are free individuals responsible for our lives." Apparently, then, college students will enjoy "personal growth" by realizing through sociology that they are not free and are not responsible for their lives. And what, we might ask, is the problem with holding such a "common sense" view? The trouble, it tells us, is that "we may be more quick to praise successful people as superior." The second point of "personal growth" offered by sociology to entice students to study it is that "Sociology helps us learn more about the world around us so that we can pursue our goals more effectively." Here is the autonomous individual being set free from social constraint to live as she or he pleases: "We have a say in how to play our cards, but it is society that deals us the hand. The more we understand the game, the better players we will be." So, apparently, academic learning for instrumental advantage in a competitive and potentially disadvantaging "society" is another form of "personal growth."

The third advantage of sociology is explicitly activist: sociology "empowers us" to become "more effective citizens," in that it "turns a private problem . . . into a public issue (a lack of good jobs)." After learning sociology, "we may decide to support society as it is, or we may set out with others to change it." Guess which of these options students, after reading this textbook, are going to know they ought to choose (assuming they have free choice)? The fourth stated sociological contribution to "personal growth" is that it "helps us live in a diverse world" by encouraging us "to think critically about" "our own way of life as 'right,' 'natural,' and 'better.'" Presumably, cultural relativism (discussed in the text's following chapter) rules out genuine moral judgments about any culture; at least the text offers no help for thinking about cultures' "strengths," as it calls them. Thus, sociology students are left criticizing what they *thought* was right and good, yet lacking help in better determining what really *is* right and good. That nicely positions them to be susceptible to recruitment into sociology's (to some students, at least) compelling sacred-spiritual-moral-political-ideological project that the textbook promotes.

In sum, sociology's value to undergraduate students in a nutshell is that it (1) disabuses their common-sense views of freedom and responsibility (and then we wonder why all the binge drinking and date rape), (2) turns students into "better [game] players" who "pursue . . . goals more effective" (and then we wonder why so many want to be business majors), (3) "empowers" students to "set out with others to change" society (which is the hook for sociology-major prospects), and (4) causes students to doubt the value of their own cultural ways of life, thus paving the way for a tolerant multiculturalism (elaborated subsequently on page 51 of the text). With that kind of impressive (secular) personal growth program, who needs religion?

Starting on page 9, the textbook then introduces a standard rhetorical move, found in most introductory textbooks, that I call the "implicit progress narrative." This rhetorical move works by pretending to be simply telling a factual story, while in fact all along using subtle discursive cues to make clear who and what is normatively better and worse, which side the reader should prefer and embrace. The basic form of the implicit progress narrative is, "In the (bad) old days, people believed or did A, but that was displaced as more recent (rational, free) people came to believe or do B." Explaining the origins of sociology as embedded in the transformations of modernity, students thus read the following observations in this textbook:

- "We see a shift in focus from people's moral duties to God and king to the pursuit of self-interest."
- "Philosophers now [compared to (allegedly) having no ideas of human rights before] spoke of *personal liberty* and

individual rights," including "life, liberty, and the pursuit of happiness" (italics original).

- "During the Middle Ages, most people [A] . . . But by the end of the eighteenth century [B]."
- "The French Revolution . . . was an even greater break with political and social tradition," producing (quoting Tocqueville) "nothing short of the regeneration of the whole human race."
- "The earliest *theological* stage" then "gave way to a *metaphysical* stage," after which "the scientific stage" took over, which applied "the scientific approach . . . to the study of society," which took form in sociology (italics in original).
- "The new industrial economy, enormous cities, and the fresh political ideas" led to the development of sociology.

On the surface, this is all pure historical description. In context and presentation, however, the new is clearly superior to the old. Who, after all, wants moral duties to God and king? Who wants to live in a theological stage when we can instead have a scientific stage? Who doesn't want modern liberty and rights? Who could possibly resist what is "new" and "fresh"? In the old (superstitious) days, the Holy Spirit used to cause human "regeneration," but now our modern political revolutions have brought us an "even greater" break (notice the normative ambiguity in the word "greater") with the past that has led to "the regeneration of the whole human race." And, isn't it great that sociology, of all disciplines, was born the fortuitous academic child of all of these progressive historical changes?[28] Early

28. Here we are also told in a footnote that, to "reflect the . . . diversity of our society," the "traditional" dating expression "before Christ" (B.C.) will be displaced by the more neutral "before the common era" (BCE), and that "in the year of our Lord" (*anno Domini,* A.D.) will be replaced by "common era" (CE). Roger that. (Yet can anyone explain why the calculated birth of Jesus Christ remains the defining moment for the start of the "common era," thus still having us follow the Gregorian calendar [Pope

sociologists, like Auguste Comte and Karl Marx, the students are then told, "were more interested in imagining the ideal society than they were in studying society as it really was. . . . They hoped that the new discipline of sociology would not just help us understand society but also to change it toward greater justice." Imagine that.

For the next many pages, readers are then tortured with a completely outdated and misleading yet standard introductory presentation of "sociological theory" in artificial three-part form. Describing a theoretical world that actually never existed in sociology, yet some simplistic semblance of which *might* have existed in, say, 1970, we read: "Sociologists make use of three theoretical approaches: the structural-functionalist approach, the social-conflict approach, and the symbolic-interaction approach." This is simply false, as every literate sociologist today knows. So, for present purposes, we must ask: Why does nearly every published introductory-sociology textbook explain sociological theory through a gross misrepresentation of what "sociologists make use of," despite having had repeated chances (in the case of this particular textbook, 11 editions of "enhancement"[29]) to improve on their truthfulness? The answer cannot be that students cannot handle an accurate, basic depiction of sociological theory today, since it's not that complicated.[30]

The answer instead is that this antiquated and misleading mode of presentation optimizes the text's ability to present sociology's sacred project in the most attractive terms, yet in a context that

Gregory's], the logic of which was first conceived by the Christian monk Dionysius Exiguus in 525 A.D., I mean CE? For that matter, do people realize that the language of "common" here, as a generic way to get the theological words "Christ" and "Lord" out of public discourse, actually came not from secular sources but from a nineteenth-century religious Jewish reckoning of calendric time?)

29. Inside front cover flap.

30. Even if it were, imagine an introductory physics, biology, or economics textbook taking the approach that what it says about its discipline's theory is actually false, at best a half-century out of date, but that will have to be good enough for a college class.

appears to involve a smart analytic comparison of alternative theories. The underlying narrative is this: Structural-functionalism is one option, but it is dated and conservative, so of not much value. The social-conflict approach, by contrast, hits the nail on the head, even if it is a bit incomplete here and there. And symbolic-interactionism offers another perspective that is often helpful at the "micro" level, especially for seeing how social conflict (and discrimination, exploitation, etc.) happens on the ground, even though it too is a bit incomplete. That story is the subtext beneath the text.

Let us see this in action in this textbook. Structural-functionalism is (of course, as always, even though there is no necessary theoretical reason for that) presented first and very briefly (in four paragraphs here). It is then given this "critical review": "By focusing attention on social stability and unity, critics point out, structural-functionalism ignores inequalities of social class, race, ethnicity, and gender, which cause tensions and conflict. In general, its focus on stability at the expense of conflict makes this approach somewhat conservative." So functionalism is taken out to the junkyard, and we read next that "sociologists developed the social-conflict approach . . . as a critical response." Hooray! (Except that this is complete 1960s-centered bunk, since Karl Marx and many other "conflict theorists" obviously wrote well before Talcott Parsons and Robert K. Merton, even before Emile Durkheim and Herbert Spencer, with whom functionalism's origins are associated.)

Here things gets more exciting, however, since the social-conflict approach is all about "how factors such as class, race, ethnicity, gender, and age are linked to inequality in terms of money, power, education, and social prestige." In this section, students are taught about ongoing conflict of "the rich in relation to the poor, white people in relation to people of color, and men in relation to women." They read about "how schooling reproduces class inequality" and how "young people from privileged families get the best schooling," "with schools justifying the practice in terms of individual merit." Never fear, however, since, "many sociologists use social-conflict analysis not just to understand society but also to reduce inequality"—citing Karl Marx that "The philosophers have only interpreted the world, in various ways; the point, however, is to change it." This section then proceeds to describe "the gender-conflict approach," feminist theory, and "the race-conflict approach." Readers are then told that "all chapters of this book consider the importance of gender and gender inequality." Having thus laid it all out in black and white (e.g., "supporters of social-conflict analysis . . . [believe] that all theoretical approaches have political consequences"), readers are then asked, in a special "Check Your Learning" section, this insipid question: "Why do you think sociologists characterize the social-conflict approach as 'activist?'"[31] (Is it any wonder, with this level of intellectual challenge, why most of the smartest undergraduate students major in disciplines other than sociology?)

Next, the text transitions to a brief summary of "the symbolic-interaction approach," which, however, it unfortunately confuses with social constructionism—as if Goffman and Stryker were the same as Berger and Luckmann—by emphasizing (the philosophically ludicrous assertions) that "society is nothing more than the reality that people construct for themselves as they interact with one another" and "We create 'reality.'" (At least "reality" was put in quotation marks here, although why so and what it means are never explained.) The main problem with the symbolic-interactionist perspective is then said to be that it "risks overlooking . . . structural factors such as class, gender, and race."

The three ways that sociologists allegedly "use theory" are then "applied" to the case of sports, the discussion of which, after a brief

---

31. Above it, a special "Thinking about Diversity: Race, Class, and Gender" box (one of 20 in the textbook) explains that the early American black sociologist W. E. B. Du Bois "saw sociology as a key to solving society's problems, especially racial inequality."

look at how structural functionalism thinks (inadequately), tells us that "throughout history, men have dominated the world of sports" and "our society long excluded people of color from professional sports." We further learn that, although things have changed for females in "the Olympics and Little League," "even today, women still take the back seat to men;" and that, although Jackie Robinson crossed the "color line" into Major League Baseball, "racial discrimination still exists in professional sports." Sociology thus teaches that "the vast profits sports generate are controlled by a small number of people—predominantly white men. In sum, sports in our country are bound up with inequalities based on gender, race, and wealth." That, then, is most college students' gateway into sociological theory.

The next section compares positivist sociology, interpretive sociology, and critical sociology. Two of the three, it turns out, can serve sociology's sacred mission. Positivist sociology can tell us, for instance that the idea that "Differences in the behavior of females and males are just 'human nature'" is "wrong." What happens in delivery rooms of hospitals (for just one example) might suggest otherwise. But the falsity of the common view, the textbook explains, is confirmed by two arguments. First, we are told, "much of what we call 'human nature' is constructed by the society in which we live." (Just ignore that the "much of" qualification here opens the door back up to some sex differences given in human nature, and, more basically, that the argument does not even logically prove the point, since the claim about social constructionism could be true and behavioral differences between men and women could still be in part biologically based.)[32] Second, we are assured, "we know this because researchers have found that definitions of 'feminine' and

---

32. Not to mention that that "evidence" has little to do with positivism, which all of this is allegedly illustrating.

'masculine' change over time and vary from one society to another."
(This too is a defective argument, since such "definitions" are ontologically different things than the sex-different "behaviors" that
they supposedly show have no grounding in human nature.) Also
shown here to be "not true" is the belief that "the United States is a
middle-class society in which most people are more or less equal."
Even the idea that "people marry because they are in love" is also
proved by positivist sociology to be "not exactly" true. (Unfortunately, again, the argument against this idea—that "many social
rules guide the selection of mates"—doesn't actually prove the
point at all, since obviously rules can guide the choices of people
who still marry for love.)[33]

The conclusion of this exercise (supposedly) illustrating positivist sociology's contribution: "We have all been brought up hear-
ing many widely accepted 'truths'. . . . As adults, we need to evaluate
more critically what we see, read, and hear. Sociology can help us
do that." Amen. (If only sociology did that with its own textbooks.)
The remainder of the discussion about positivism then uses poverty to illustrate the fact that "correlation is not causation" and
qualifies the Weberian idea about researchers needing to be "value
free" by admitting that "we can never be completely value-free or
even aware of our biases." True. In fact, the text admonishes, with
some false humility: "Sociologists are not 'average' people: Most
are highly educated white men and women who are more politically liberal than the population as a whole. Sociologists need to remember that they, too, are influenced by their social backgrounds."
You don't say! Even so, positivist sociology is said to appeal to
scholars "who have a more conservative political view." I suppose
it is all relative.

---

33. A "box" discussion at the top of this page informs readers normatively that they need
    not worry about the problem of extramarital sex, since positivist science tells us that a
    lot less of it happens than people commonly imagine.

"Interpretive sociology" is then given a brief, three-paragraph description, ending with the empiricist comment that "subjective thoughts and feelings" are things "which scientists tend to dismiss because they are difficult to measure" (but which interpretive scholars nonetheless focus upon). More space (naturally) is then given to "critical sociology," which is presented as "the study of society that focuses on the need for social change." This way of doing sociology negates the idea that "society should exist in its present form," objects to "inequality," wishes to "change [society] in the direction of democracy and social justice," and rejects the idea of value-free science in favor of emphasizing "instead that sociologists should be activists in pursuit of greater social equality." This approach, we are told, in case it is not already obvious, "appeals to those whose politics ranges from liberal to radical left."[34]

The remainder of this textbook's first chapter spends one section pointing out the various ways that "research is affected by gender" and the many scholarly dangers of acting "as if only men's activities are important, ignoring what women do;" and concluding a very brief discussion about research ethics with "tips on . . . sensitivity to outsiders" (such as Hispanics) "in a diverse society such as our own." Finally, in a discussion of research methods, we learn the following. First, the Zimbardo "Stanford Prison Experiment" (which illustrates the experimental method) tells us that "prison violence is rooted in the social character of the jails themselves, not in the personalities of individual guards and prisoners." (Having ruled out a priori the idea of human nature with a very bad argument some pages previously, the more obvious interpretation of the Zimbardo

---

34. On p. 21, we then read this erroneous claim, which imposes on sociology a nonexistent order and logic: "The positivist orientation is linked to the structural-functional approach, . . . the interpretive orientation to the symbolic-interaction approach, . . . and the critical orientation to the social-conflict approach." The misrepresentation of facts here boggles the mind.

prison-experiment study has thus been made invisible—namely, that most or all human beings have a natural tendency to violently dominate others, so that all they need is a social environment that allows their natural aggressive dominance to express itself and it does.[35] But deprived of that simple interpretation, we are left with "sociological" assertions the plausibility of which hinges on the ambiguities of the phrases "rooted in" and "social character," and the insertion of the key word "personalities." Prematurely and probably falsely, then, do these sociologists draw the conclusion that the experimental evidence "supports the hypothesis" that "the prison setting itself . . . is the cause of the prison violence"—even assuming that any cogent account could be offered for how a "setting" per se can be the "cause" of human actions, which I doubt.)

Second, a study of African-American elites (which illustrates survey research at work) "concluded that, despite the improving social standing of African Americans, black people in the United States still suffer the sting of racial hostility," that many highly successful blacks do not "escape the sting of racism," and that many successful blacks report "fearing that race might someday undermine their success." We are then shown that William Foote Whyte's classic study, *Street Corner Society* (which illustrates the method of participant observation), taught him that "common stereotypes [about a slum] were wrong. . . . Most people worked hard, many were quite successful, and some even boasted of sending children to college."

Then, since sociology specializes in generalizations, this chapter then heads down the finish line by explaining "how the generalizations made by sociologists differ from the common stereotypes we hear every day" (the answer, in short, is that sociology is right because it is based on "facts;" stereotypes are wrong). Therefore,

---

35. The University of Maryland Government and Political scholar Fred Alford makes this alternative point clearly and forcefully in *What Evil Means to Us* (1997, Ithaca: Cornell University Press, pp. 24–30).

"a sociology classroom is a good place to get at the truth behind common stereotypes" (the caption under a photo is of three agitated students—two women and one black man—apparently pressing their professor for, in fact nearly raising a protest to get at, "the truth").

Finally, this first chapter returns to the thematic query with which it opened: Why do couples marry? Apparently assuming that readers are by now brain dead (which is highly plausible), this inquiry offers this "HINT": "Consider: (1) rules about same-sex and other-sex marriage, (2) laws defining the number of people who may marry, (3) the importance of race and ethnicity, (4) the importance of social class, (5) the importance of age, (6) the importance of social exchange (what each partner offers the other)."[36] A large photo of Ellen DeGeneres showing off her engagement ring on the hand of her fiancée adorns the spread, with the caption:

> In 1997, during the fourth season of her hit TV show, *Ellen,*
> Ellen DeGeneres "came out" as a lesbian, which put her on the
> cover of *Time* magazine. Since then, she has been an activist on
> behalf of gay and lesbian issues. Following California's brief legalization of same-sex marriage in 2008, she married her longtime girlfriend, Australian actress Portia de Rossi.

This completes my summary of the (not very) hidden curriculum in the first 32 pages of this best-selling sociology textbook. What we have learned from it about the discipline of sociology is the following. Sociology is obsessed with same-sex relationships,

---

36. The first "hint" is of course American sociology's current *cause célèbre;* the second indirectly softens up readers for what logically comes next, namely polyamorous marriage (as long as "the threesome or more are deeply in love," which seems to be the only criterion defining the basis of marriage in this text, see p. 2); the remaining four hints are standard sociological variables and social cleavages defining structures of inequality.

marriage, and legal struggles. Sociology is fixated on socioeco-nomic inequalities, especially around race, social class, and gender, but also around age, ethnicity, sexual orientation, and family struc-ture. Men dominate women, and whites dominate blacks. Sociol-ogy cares deeply about social and cultural diversity. Sociology is at its best when revealing the social conflicts that erupt from social inequalities. The coming of the modern (secular) world, which gave birth to sociology, is a good thing. Sociology is highly skepti-cal about common sense, tradition, human nature, and stereotypes, and seeks to replace those with its own systematic, scientific knowl-edge. People "construct" "reality" through their interactions. Peo-ple's ideas about what is true are culturally relative constructions which they should criticize and doubt. A truth exists that sociol-ogy can reveal. Human free will is largely if not entirely an illusion. People should exercise their wills in order to pursue their goals more effectively. People's actions are caused by the "social charac-ter" of "settings" rather than by features or capacities of the people. Sociologists are not average people, but more educated and liberal. Sociology shapes public policy and foments social change through empowerment, movements of change, and influencing public policy. Sociology cares about social justice and democracy. One of the three major (and best) ways to do sociology uses academic study as a kind of activism to foster social change and equality. This, in short, represents the first-chapter textbook view of American so-ciology, which barely hides the nature of its sacred project.

For readers who know more about sociology and its scholarship, and what makes for an effective logical argument, here is what read-ing this first chapter also tells us. First, sociology does not care if the statistics of one of its own big (feminist) studies were grossly wrong and discredited by other skeptical scholars, since it is ap-parently okay to continue to quote those studies as authoritative even 15 years later (more on this below). Second, we should be introducing undergraduate students to sociology by immediately telling them things about theory in the discipline that every working sociologist knows are false. Third, we sociologists should feel free to make assertions about facts to students based on "arguments" that in no way actually logically justify those assertions, which colleagues in other disciplines could and would tear to shreds if they knew we were asserting them. Fourth, even though we in sociology embrace and advance an obviously normative-political-moral-spiritual agenda (that is often quite different from that of most Americans), we are justified in trying to cloak that for our students behind a discourse that seems balanced, scientific, and self-critical.

I could continue the exact same kind of analysis of the next 465 pages of this one sociology textbook. The results, however, would continue to repeat what I have presented above. What we saw in one chapter shows up in all of the chapters. If I continued my analysis of this textbook, we would find, for example, that the vast majority of the rest of the text focuses on cultural and economic inequalities and other social problems. Even in chapters one might expect to be "dry," such as that about "Groups and Organizations," the text's focus remains on concerns most dear to sociology's sacred project, like the threats of authoritarianism, conformity, groupthink, coercive organizations, oligarchies, "patterns of privilege and exclusion" by race and gender, organizational threats of personal privacy, and women's disadvantages vis-à-vis "old boy" networks, while the role of women in organizations is valorized: "While some men initially opposed women's presence in the executive office, it is now clear that women bring particular strengths to the job, including leadership flexibility and communication skills. Thus, some analysts speak of women offering a 'female advantage.'"[37]

37. Pp. 118–165, quote from p. 133.

"Sex and Sexuality" as topics are privileged with the entire sixth chapter's devotion to them, while family and religion are crammed together in Chapter 13. The former chapter spends much space discussing inter-sexed people, transsexuals, bisexuals, the sexual revolution, premarital sex, sexual orientation, the gay rights movement (including a story about whether gay high schoolers could go to their proms), homophobia, queer theory, hooking up (which has "advantages" and "disadvantages" that readers are encouraged to weigh), sex workers, sexual inequalities, the social control of sexuality (such as medieval chastity belts), the sexual freedoms of Melanesian cultures, date rape (about which is reported the insightful sociological finding that rape leaves "emotional and psychological scars"), "adultery" (about which we are told, however, "sociologists prefer the more neutral term extramarital sex"), abortion (emphasizing the "angry confrontations" and murders of abortion doctors by the pro-life side, and ending with the compelling rationale of the pro-choice side[38]), and American men's demand for prostitutes. All of this includes uses of the "implicit progress narrative" method

38. "Anyone who has read the papers in recent years knows about the angry confrontations at abortion clinics across North America. Some opponents have even targeted and killed doctors who carry out abortions;" then on the next page, "Pro-choice advocates are ... committed to the position that women must have control over their own bodies. If pregnancy decides the course of women's lives, women will never be able to compete with men on equal terms, whether it is on campus or in the workplace. Therefore, access to legal, safe abortion is a necessary condition to women's full participation in society" (pp. 164–165). Elsewhere, the book discusses "the antiabortion movement" as tending to make women feel guilty, with how people talk as more determinative of women's self-evaluations than the actual experience of abortion itself; this includes pro-life assumptions that are expressed among medical personnel: "The words that doctors and nurses use guide whether a woman having an abortion defines the experience in positive or negative terms.... Nurses and doctors who talk about 'the baby' encourage the antiabortion framing of abortion and provoke grief and guilt.... Believing that what she had done was wrong... Gina [one research subject] actively called out the feeling of guilt—in part ... to punish herself." By contrast, the pro-choice position frames abortion as involving "pregnancy tissue," "the contents of the uterus," "products of conception," and even "extra cells [in the] body," which avoids guilt feelings (pp. 106–107).

noted above ("Many people in the United States *still* view sexual conduct as an important indicator of personal morality," "the ongoing sexual revolution is evident in the fact that there is now greater acceptance of premarital sex as well as increasing tolerance for various sexual orientations," and "in recent decades, public opinion about sexual orientation has shown a remarkable change").

The part-chapter on family emphasizes that "families are changing;" that family is (only) a "symbolic institution;" that race, class, and gender "are powerful forces that shape marriage and family life;" and that "alternative family forms" bring "increasing diversity" to family life—concluding with a "controversy and debate" box on "Should We Save the Traditional Family?" (ending with Judith Stacy's argument that "Traditional Families are the Problem"). That section finishes by telling students to prepare for more divorce, more family diversity, men's greater involvement in child rearing, economic forces altering family life, and new reproductive technologies. These are just a few more examples of the ways that the interests and norms of sociology's sacred project are manifest in this sociology text. I could continue presenting similar examples from this text for a long time, but in the interest of space, I will leave it at that.

I could also conduct the same kind of analysis of the other best-selling introductory sociology textbooks, and again, the results would be extremely similar. Contradicting their claims to the contrary[39], these textbooks are almost identical to each other, so we would not observe significant variance across them, but instead only more sociological homogeneity. Rather than wearying my readers with much more of the same, however, I will summarize by saying this. The

---

39. For example, Kerry Ferris and Jill Stein (201) explain why they wrote their "alternative" textbook in 2008: "It is time for a new Introductory Sociology textbook that is really new," which theirs purports to be but in fact mostly repeats the same "repetitive formulas, stodgy styles, and seemingly irrelevant materials" that they (rightly) critique in other texts (p. xix).

best-selling sociology textbooks consistently and very predictably convey to readers the strong message that sociology is committed to a very particular project. They also employ a variety of discursive strategies to convince—I would say indoctrinate—students into accepting and ideally embracing its particular assumptions, commitments, perspectives, and mission. Far from being merely informative, balanced presentations of what sociology has learned scientifically about society, these introductory textbooks function as recruiting tools and re-socialization manuals for the movement that is American sociology's sacred project, as I described it above—all being assigned as required reading for courses that are typically mandatory in a limited menu of core-curriculum graduation requisites, not to mention embarrassingly dumbed down and exploitatively overpriced (and kept that way through the publication of incessantly "new" editions). If sociologists had any intellectual and moral integrity, in my view, they would refuse to impose these textbooks on their students, and instead assign for required reading real sociological books and articles. I fear, however, that the compelling yet invisible nature of their own disciplinary spiritual project prevents them from even seeing the problems I am trying to point out here. Besides, assigning textbooks reduces the work it takes to teach a course really well.

REVEALING ANECDOTES

Now let us examine some less systematic but still I think revealing illustrations of American sociology's deep spiritual project at work.[40] The *sacred* nature—and not simply scientific, mundane, utilitarian, or instrumentally political character—of American

---

40. For a related and more systematic analysis of similar themes, see George Yancey, 2011, *Compromising Scholarship: Religious and Political Bias in American Higher Education*, Waco, TX: Baylor University Press.

sociology's defining project is revealed by the visionary features of its interests and manifest in the intense reactions and sometimes vehemence that sociologists express when that project seems violated or threatened, even in small ways. This, of course, is what we expect sociologically, when it comes to any part of human life that is believed to have a *sacred* quality, as American sociology's sacred project does. In such situations, believers in sociology's project "show themselves," to use a fine Southern expression, for the ultimate sacred ideals to which they are committed in it.[41] Again, nobody, I am sure, has conducted or could conduct a systematic study of such features and reactions to empirically "prove" my point. I trust that some anecdotes recounted from my own personal experience among fellow sociologists will add to the above evidence and help make the point sufficiently for readers who are also familiar with these matters. The following anecdotes mostly concern issues of either family-gender-sexuality or religion, both of which are areas of importance for sociology's sacred project. Here goes.

Once, while teaching a graduate seminar on qualitative research methods, one of the students, a lesbian, insisted, during a larger discussion on the purpose of sociological research, that, as she informed us, "I am not in my research simply to win same-sex rights. I am in it to overthrow the entire Judeo-Christian cultural and social system."[42] It was a not-inappropriate point to contribute in the context of our discussion. But as a claim about professional

---

41. Referring to situations in which people in unexpected or stressful social situations inadvertently and often somewhat embarrassingly reveal more about their true feelings or thoughts than they ordinary would prefer to reveal, disrupting their controlled presentations of self in a way that shows their true colors or positions—an expression I learned living in North Carolina while working at UNC-Chapel Hill.

42. In most cases here, I leave specific persons unnamed, since my point does not concern this or that person but rather the larger project, culture, and movement that sociology is. Readers determined to identify names can in some cases find them on the Internet. Only in cases that have been highly public and familiar, where pretending to maintain anonymity would be silly, do I name names.

THE SACRED PROJECT OF AMERICAN SOCIOLOGY

motives, I thought it revealing. Going far beyond an interest in simply learning about society through scholarship and educating others, this student was after a visionary and comprehensive revolution of a system that she viewed as violating the most important human goods, values, feelings, desires, and purposes imaginable. Her struggle was not simply political, but ultimately spiritual, in the sense I define above. And the profession of sociology was her means for accomplishing that goal.[43]

Another graduate-student story: In a different graduate seminar, another student recurrently brought up certain conservative groups, such as the evangelical "pro-family ministry" organization, Focus on the Family, led then by the child and family psychologist, Dr. James Dobson. She was somewhat interested in conducting research on this group. Focus on the Family had a huge following then among conservative Christians, and probably beyond, bolstered by a popular radio program led by and bestselling books and a popular newsletter published by Dobson. Focus on the Family was also indirectly involved in "pro-family" politics, insofar as Dobson encouraged listeners and readers to "defend the traditional family" with their voting and letters and calls to political representatives. It struck me odd that this ex-Catholic, very politically liberal student would be so knowledgeable about this group and others like it. I asked her why and how so. She replied quickly with a sly smile, "It's important to know our enemies. I keep a close eye on them."

43. Such statements pop up in sociology with regularity. In a recent sociology blog debate about the possible value of one particular philosophy of social science, one prominent sociologist admitted the following: "I'm never going to be an expert on this, but I know philosophy is important, so I realize this debate might someday affect sociology in an important way. When and if it does, my (opening) position on it . . . will start with weights based on the research I see that engages the debate, from what I know. Maybe (in all seriousness) that's because I'm an ignorant American sociologist obsessed with problem solving, by which I mean providing *solutions that serve my thinly-concealed leftism.*" http://orgtheory.wordpress.com/2013/09/04/a-word-on-critical-realism/#comment-134,805 (as of September 9, 2013).

Enemies. That is not the language of science, except when referring to diseases or ignorance. Nor is it the language of the methodologically empathetic ethnographic field-worker seeking to understand a radically different tribe or other social group from within its own native cultural worlds. "Enemies" is the language of war, of armed combat with lethal intent, of political struggle as a metaphorical extension of war, and (among some kinds of religious people) of "spiritual warfare." This graduate student was not into sociology—perhaps even conducting research on Focus on the Family—simply in order to systematically study, better understand, and theorize the various ways that social life works. She had a project. She was an activist. Her interests were of course political and ideological. But they were more than that. They were sacred and spiritual, driving her into sociology as a way to pursue her project. What she was after concerned not simply political power, but matters to her of ultimate meaning, value, and goodness over which was worth monitoring and fighting enemies.

Another example: The 2002 program of the annual meeting of the ASA included an "Author Meets Critics" session focused on the then-recently-published book about the many benefits of marriage, the lead author of which was a very highly regarded University of Chicago sociologist and demographer. The book presented a very impressive, empirically grounded argument for how and why marriage typically benefits both partners, drawing on hundreds of the best scholarly findings from decades of serious research. Two demographer critics on the panel engaged the author in a smart and fair discussion—not a surprise to those familiar with social demographers.[44] But the third critic, a sociologist, sex therapist, and popular sex book author whose public view is totally pro-sexual-revolution,

---

44. Who straddle a dual identity as demographers and sociologists, and many (but not all) of whom tend to be less ideological and more scientifically oriented.

excoriated the author. *"You have betrayed us!"* she castigated the author. An eyewitness on the front line of the event reported to me that this critic "literally frothed at the mouth," denouncing the author for writing a book that was "politically motivated" and accusing her of "cherry picking" findings that selectively supported her conclusions. The book's author herself later recalled to me that being branded "politically incorrect" in that way by this critic and other sociologists in the audience and beyond put an end to her involvement with the ASA as an elected officer. In fact, anyone who has carefully read this book and knows the author's scholarly credentials realizes that this critic's condemnation was preposterously ridiculous.

How then might we explain her over-the-top reaction on a public stage? Not, I think, by assuming that the critic is an emotionally unstable person. In fact, she is an experienced public speaker, more than capable of handling herself well on stage and on camera. The explanation, I suggest, is instead that this book violated the sacred character of the sacred project to which this sociologist was and is absolutely committed, something that was intolerable, no matter what the mountains of empirical evidence said or how deservedly respectable was the book's scholar. The book suggested that traditional marriage—which at least some sociologists consider a form of legalized patriarchal indentured servitude—is a generally good social institution beneficial to most spouses. The book also left undecided, because definitive research findings on the topic simply did not exist, the question of whether same-sex marriage was similarly beneficial. So, *"You have betrayed us!"* tells it all. Provoked was the rage of one devoted to a sectarian sacred quest unleashed on another presumed to be a fellow-activist but who proved traitorously unfaithful to that quest.[45]

45. A similar story ought to be told about the absurdly irate reactions by sociology colleagues (who actually had nothing substantive to say) in reply to University of Texas at Austin sociologist Norval Glenn's smashing 1997 report on very real and obvious ideological biases in sociology of marriage and family textbooks, "Closed Hearts,

More: In 2003, I teamed up with a fantastic Jewish–Unitarian Universalist colleague and friend working in the Department of Religious Studies to found an academic undergraduate minor at the University of North Carolina at Chapel Hill in the academic study of Christianity. Our proposal was to coordinate existing faculty and course resources already in place at the university to offer a new minor for students interested in learning more in the humanities and social sciences about Christian history, culture, theology, and social influences. Even though the minor was topically about Christianity, it was constructed to be entirely academic and nonconfessional in every way. According to university regulations, the minor had to have a "home" in an already-established department. The obvious home for such a minor was Religious Studies. But most faculty in that department took the view that all religions expressed the highest insights and aspirations of humanity—all religions, that is, except one (guess which!). So they were not interested in supporting the minor. We turned then to my own department, sociology. Most of my colleagues there then—being good, scientific neo-positivists, which makes a difference in such matters—were among the most professional, fair-minded sociologists in the discipline, in my experience. So I was hopeful that, even if just as a favor to me, and despite many of them being hard-core secularists, they would approve departmental "ownership" of our proposed minor. My hopes were well founded. All it took was a tweak of the minor's name from "Christian Studies" to "Christianity and Culture," to which I happily agreed, and the majority of my colleagues approved sociology as its official departmental home. But one comment made

Closed Minds: The Textbook Story of Marriage." I remember being perplexed by them at the time, but I regrettably did not document then; Glenn's untimely death in 2011 unfortunately prevents me from gathering sufficient documented evidence about the incident now to report the facts in detail here—though perhaps someone I currently do not know has documentation and can make them public as a contribution to continuing discussion about these issues.

by one colleague during the faculty meeting was especially revealing, I thought, about the larger backdrop of assumptions and commitments defining our discipline more broadly.

To understand the comment's full ironic significance, one has
to know that this colleague was the founder and ardent activist-
advocate for another minor also housed in and supported by our
department, the minor in "Social and Economic Justice" (of which
I was also a supporter). Clearly uncomfortable with the notion that
sociology might actually lend even minimal aid to the development
of the academic study of Christianity, of all things, and seeming
to be searching for some way to derail its approval, this colleague
posed this searching question to all of the deliberating faculty: "But
isn't the study of Christianity *too normative*?" Too normative? The
university supported Women's Studies, Africana Studies, postmod-
ernist deconstruction in Communication Studies, her own minor,
and who knows what else. But the academic, non-confessional
study of Christianity—one of the major influences on Western
civilization—was "too normative." I did not know how to respond
properly. Thankfully, one of my more sensible (totally secular)
colleagues with a puzzlingly annoyed look on his face asked the
obvious question: "Well, isn't Social and Economic Justice pretty
normative too?" That ended that discussion. The votes were cast
and our minor was up and running.

On the face of it, this episode appears to somewhat discredit my
thesis in this book. As far as I know, only a handful of my colleagues
were unhappy about "Christianity" having anything to do with the
department. Most were reasonable about the proposal. But the faculty in my department then was also a well-known outlier in being
ideologically moderate for those of a sociology program (that being
commonly attributed to its being in the South, to numerous of our
faculty being students of business and entrepreneurs, and to others
on our faculty being social demographers—who tend to be relatively

EVIDENCE

atheoretical and scientistically non-ideological). In most other U.S. sociology departments, my minor proposal would not have stood a chance. But even in this kind of mostly sane context, the question was seriously ventured by a social-and-economic-justice academic-activist, "Isn't the study of Christianity *too normative*?"

What did that actually mean? Simply that treating Christianity as an object of serious academic attention somehow threatened to violate the sacred project of American sociology—of which this particular questioning colleague was an archetypical representative and apostle—enough that some intervention, no matter how illogical, bigoted, and based on a double standard, had to be ventured to stop it. But why would that be? Well, Christianity is a religion (strike one) that defined the reigning sacred heart of western Christendom for well more than a millennium (strike two) and that teaches metaphysics and moral standards that challenge many of the assumptions, values, and commitments of sociology's sacred project (a big strike three). Most of my good colleagues were willing to accommodate my request, even if they perhaps naturally did not love it, because, I think, they wanted to be supportive of me personally and because they realized there were no reasonable grounds whatsoever for opposing the proposal. But one most seriously devoted to our discipline's sacred project, understood by her in quite sectarian terms, somehow found a way nonetheless to overcome those constraints and ask the ludicrous question. Given the entire context and situation, her objection I think was the local exception that proved the general rule about sociology as a discipline—namely, that it is driven by a powerful, pre-scientific, sacred project and so not particularly subject to the constraints of evidence or reason when they seem to challenge that project.

I am privy to most of the details of the following events, because I personally know some of the people involved; but, given how politically explosive they were, and having been asked not to stir up trouble now that things are largely settled, I must write about them here in the most general terms. Not very long ago, a quite well-published sociologist with a PhD from a top sociology program in an Ivy League university came up, according to the standard schedule for such matters, for tenure and promotion at the university in which he or she was employed. This was and is a nationally well-regarded research university, but its sociology program has been historically weak and was not highly ranked. This scholar's record of publication was stronger than the majority of his or her colleagues who were evaluating him or her for tenure and promotion. Unfortunately for this scholar, he or she also happened to be a member of a major religious body in the United States that takes some public positions that are at odds with those entailed in sociology's spiritual project; he or she was also what we might call a conservative. Nonetheless, this scholar had published articles and books in the best journals and with the best publishers. Any objective observer would have definitely recommended promotion and tenure. This scholar's faculty colleagues, however, did not (although some did argue against their majority "no" vote). During the faculty meeting where his or her case was discussed, some colleagues actually explicitly raised concerns both about this person's religious commitments and the political/cultural conservatism—so it has been leaked by persons in attendance. The fact that those details ought to be irrelevant to tenure-and-promotion decisions and that raising them in a formal faculty meeting was actually *illegal* did not seem to cross the minds of most of the faculty in the meeting at the time. The majority of faculty voted to recommend denying this scholar tenure and promotion.

The case was, according to proper procedure, sent up to the Dean and the Dean's committee for review and recommendation. The Dean and the Dean's committee supported the sociology faculty's decision, recommending denial of tenure and promotion to the university Provost. A controversy started brewing and lawyers were becoming involved. Only because the vote to deny tenure was on the face of it preposterous and because the Provost knew that the university would not only be sued and but would deservedly lose the case, the Provost overruled the sociology faculty, the Dean, and the Dean's committee, and granted this sociologist tenure and promotion. Needless to say, to continue to make this department his or her professional home was for this scholar extremely awkward and uncomfortable, despite his or her case being vindicated by the university's Provost. By now it is mostly water under the bridge, everyone carries on with whatever levels of unhappiness and discomfort he or she happens to feel, and life goes on. But what might we learn from this episode? This scholar's personal religious and political commitments so threatened to violate the sacred project in which the majority of this sociology faculty were so invested that they were prepared to engage in university standards-violating and even illegal measures to prevent him or her from becoming a permanent member of their department. Heterodoxy was polluting. The offending party had to be rooted out and excluded. Those at times are some of the ways that the deep commitments to sociology's sacred project are expressed.

Next comes a more mundane anecdote. At any public presentation in any academic department that is at least moderately functional—in seminars, colloquia, and job talks, and so on—various of the participants engage in diverse kinds of (Goffmanesque) presentations of self that represent and affirm their own personal moral identities and confirm group solidarity. One of the ways that this identity and solidarity work is accomplished—especially in liminal times before and after speakers talk, including informal parts of speakers' introductions—involves off-handedly bringing up various political, ideological, and cultural topics, sometimes making a funny remark about people or groups who hold the "wrong" views about those topics, sometimes expressing serious exasperation over such people and groups, and then affirming an obviously politically correct position on the issue to wrap the matter up. Of late, I have observed, a favorite topic of such conversation among sociologists has been the Tea Party. Various thoughts about the Tea Party might be voiced, but they all add up to this identical perspective: Tea Partiers represent idiocy, social-class oppression, political injustice, economic exploitation, and sinister intentions. About this there is no room for debate or argument—otherwise, it would not be brought up in the first place (and the economists, who might see things differently, have their own department and offices on a different floor). The correct perspective is obvious and ubiquitous. On occasion, however, such ritualized exhibitions of moral identity and group solidarity are humorously (to me, at least) potentially jeopardized by momentarily bad performances. Recently, for instance, I witnessed one sociologist, while introducing a visiting speaker, who apparently had a research interest in the Tea Party, say something to the effect that they themselves were also interested in the Tea Party. Suddenly, it was realized that the statement might be mistaken as actual personal concern about and support for the Tea Party. Despite the fact that nobody in the room could have possibly imagined such a thing about this familiar colleague, the said person immediately started falling all over themselves to clarify that they in no way believed in or supported the Tea Party. One wonders why that "clarification" happened, it having in actuality been totally and obviously unnecessary. The answer is that even the possibility of risking suggesting in sociological circles that one might be even remotely "interested in" the Tea Party just might be misconstrued as actually being sympathetic to the Tea Party, which would of course be an unspeakable offense, a pollution of purity, a dark heresy for orthodox dogma. Even the possible hint of a suggestion of the possibility required an immediate retraction, a recantation of sorts, to make sure that the collective sacred project was not in any way compromised.

Another anecdote. When I was in graduate school at Harvard University during the 1980s, the sociology faculty there was joined by a scholar who studied the legal background to and socioeconomic consequences of divorce in the United States, Lenore Weitzman (in this case, there is no use trying to keep her name anonymous). Somewhere along the way, I served as a teaching assistant for her, in an undergraduate course on the family, mostly grading exams. I was impressed by her dramatic empirical findings about the economic differences in how divorce affected men and women. Men after divorce fared extremely well, apparently, while women after divorce were economically devastated. Specifically, Weitzman reported that women's standard of living *declined* by 73 percent while men's *increased* by 42 percent! I even used those amazing findings from her book to give my first-ever job-talk class lecture (to demonstrate my potential teaching abilities), which went well (I got the job). In subsequent years, however, word began leaking out that something was wrong with Weitzman's numbers.[46] The Social Science Research Council sociologist Richard Peterson was suspicious of her findings, since they were out of line with what many other previous studies had found (which should have been a clue for everyone who accepted Weitzman's numbers). Peterson wanted to replicate her findings, but Weitzman refused to make her data available to him, saying that she first wanted to

46. The following is based on Richard Peterson, 1996, "A Re-Evaluation of the Economic Consequences of Divorce," *American Sociological Review*, 61: 528–536; ASA, 1996, "ASR Features Debate Over Divorce Data," *Footnotes*, 24(5): 1, 4; Katharine Webster, 1996, "Post-Divorce Wealth Gap Was Wrong, Agrees Author," *The Seattle Times*, May 19; Felicia Lee, 1996, "Influential Study on Divorce's Impact is Said to be Flawed," *The New York Times*, May 9; and Christopher Rapp, n.d., "Lies, Damned Lies, and Lenore Weitzman," http://www.familylawwebguide.com.au/library/spca/docs/Lies%20Damned%20Lies%20and%20Lenore%20Weitzman.pdf.

correct some errors in her master computer file. Eventually, she archived her data in the Murray Research Center at Radcliffe College, but still vetoed Peterson's request to access it. After most of a decade of delay, the National Science Foundation, which had funded Weitzman's research, finally threatened to list her as ineligible for future research funding if she did not release her dataset to Peterson—so she did.

When he finally laid his hands on Weitzman's dataset, Peterson found discrepancies between the paper records out of which the computer file was constructed and the numbers in the computer file itself, "numerous inaccuracies in the data for the income variables," as well as other kinds of "problematic" data and "inconsistencies," including a large amount of missing data on the key variables.[47] Peterson corrected the errors as well as he could and replicated Weitzman's analysis. His results were massively different than Weitzman's: instead of a 73 percent decline in women's standard of living after divorce, he found, using her own data, only a 27 percent decrease; and instead of a 43 percent increase in men's standard of living after divorce, Peterson found only a 10 percent increase. "Her numbers are just not accurate," he concluded. Two other scholars doubtful of Weitzman's findings also conducted a replication study of the economic effects of divorce on men and women using more reliable General Social Survey data. They found that *both* women and men suffered economic declines after divorce—a 22 percent decline in family income for women and a 10 percent decrease in the same for men.[48] In short, Weitzman's findings were way, way off. Facing this disconfirming evidence, she finally admitted as much, blaming it on the loss of her original computer data file, an error in statistical weighting, and/or a mistake in computer programming

47. Peterson, 1996, p. 530.
48. Stroup and Pollock, 1994, "Economic Consequences of Marital Dissolution," *Journal of Divorce and Remarriage*, 22 (1–2): 37–54.

performed by a graduate student research assistant.[49] Weitzman was embarrassed, although not too much, it seems.

The important questions for present purposes are these: Why were Weitzman's original findings so widely accepted and heralded by most sociologists (including myself), other scholars, and the media? Why were the few well-established scholars who raised doubts about her findings so readily dismissed and ignored? Why were studies conducted before and after Weitzman's that reported discrepant findings also paid so little attention by many sociologists? And why did eventual revelations of her gross errors (at best) not create major disciplinary negative criticism and consequences? In retrospect, actually, we see more clearly that her original research design and data were not only not nationally representative but in fact not terribly impressive. Her study was of only 228 divorcing people in Los Angeles County in 1977–79, in which only one of the divorcing spouses was interviewed—meaning that her sample was too small to be representative of much and was, in any case, drawn from a part of the country with a distinctive legal system and culture of divorce. Her key analytic concept of "ratio of income to needs" also relied on highly questionable assumptions, including the ignoring of the value and distribution of most assets accumulated pre-divorce. And yet, with some notable exceptions[50], Weitzman's conclusions were generally warmly received and validated in sociology and by many people beyond. Her study won the

---

49. Lenore Weitzman, 1996, "The Economic Consequences of Divorce are Still Unequal," *American Sociological Review*, 61: 537–538; Webster, 1996. Peterson, however, insisted that those mistakes could not have produced the magnitude of error found in Weitzman's book (ASA, 1996, p. 4).

50. Arland Thornton, 1986, "The Fragile Family," *Family Planning Perspectives*, 18: 243–244; Frank Furstenberg, 1987, "The Divorce Dilemma: After the Revolution," *Contemporary Sociology*, 16: 556–558; Jed Abraham, 1989, "'The Divorce Revolution' Revisited: A Counter-Revolutionary Critique," *Northern Illinois Law Review*, 9: 251–298; Saul Hoffman and Greg Duncan, 1988, "What are the Economic Consequences of Divorce?," *Demography*, 25: 641–645.

ASA's 1986 Book Award for "Distinguished Contribution to Scholarship." It was reviewed in at least 22 social science journals and 11 law reviews. Weitzman's findings were cited (by 1996) in more than 170 newspaper and magazine articles, 348 social science articles, 250 law review articles, 24 state court cases, and one U.S. Supreme Court decision. Despite growing doubts expressed by colleagues, Weitzman reiterated her "73/42" statistic testifying before the U.S. Congress. Legislatures around the country also reconsidered their divorce laws in reaction to her findings. In fact, Weitzman personally took credit in 1996 for shaping 14 laws in California alone.[51] President Bill Clinton actually cited her book's findings in his 1996 budget proposal.[52] And, as I noted above, Weitzman's erroneous findings continue to be cited today without problem in the bestselling Introduction to Sociology textbook on the market, 15 years after Peterson's replication and discrediting of her work.

The answer to the questions above is that Weitzman's findings—especially the "73/42 percent gap" in standard of living between divorced men and women—provided a grand-slam hit for sociology's spiritual project that was too wonderful to be doubted or criticized. Her findings dramatically uncovered a new social problem involving a gross injustice (the unintended economic injustices of no-fault divorce laws). They showed in simple terms how women were being screwed by those bad divorce laws, while men after divorce were becoming, it seemed, "part of that 'bachelor set' again, with no responsibilities and a lot of money."[53] And the findings commended specific legal reforms targeted to make men pay—such as dramatically raising required levels of child support extracted from divorced fathers—which demonstrated that sociology could have a real, gender-equality and economic-justice impact on public policy

51. Weitzman, 1996, p. 538.
52. Peterson, 1996, p. 529; Rapp, n.d., p. 4.
53. Rapp, n.d., p. 5.

(something sociology is not used to). Journalists loved the "pop" that the astounding "73/42" statistic gave their articles, feminists loved the "hard" evidence of women once again being the victims of men's institutional exploitation, and sociologists generally liked seeing one of their own attracting so much attention in the news, courts, and legislatures. In that context, the other scholars whose research findings disputed Weitzman's were pesky dark clouds raining on the parade. Who wanted them? Weitzman had become a kind of scholarly hero in many circles—gender studies, feminist jurisprudence, women's studies, the sociology of gender, divorce-law reform movements, and the women's movement broadly. For very many, her essential discovery and its implications were still correct, even if her numbers were "not exactly right."[54] In the end, the admitted huge errors in her research—which helped shape major legal and cultural changes on divorce, including some that profoundly affected divorced men—have not hurt Weitzman's career. She is currently the Clarence J. Robinson Professor of Sociology and Law at George Mason University, Fairfax, Virginia. She meant well, it seems, and she helped advance the sacred project. So what's the big deal with untrue research findings and a questionable refusal to let skeptics gain access to her publicly funded data for 10 years?

Finally, one particularly unsavory incident that rocked the sociological boat in the summer and fall of 2012 provides a final, contrasting case demonstrating the existence and sometimes dangerous consequences of the sacred project that governs American sociology. That was the surreal reaction of many in American sociology and beyond to the publication by University of Texas at Austin sociologist Mark Regnerus of a scholarly journal article

54. Her own version of this view—namely, that we need not worry about "one statistic in a 500-page book"—is found in Weitzman, 1996; to which Richard Peterson's disclaiming reply was exactly correct (Peterson, 1996, "Statistical Errors, Faulty Conclusions, Misguided Policy: Reply to Weitzman," *American Sociological Review*, 61: 539–540).

about the well-being of U.S. adults who reported having a parent who had had one or more same-sex romantic relationships earlier in life. That article, titled "How Different are the Adult Children of Parents who Have Same-Sex Relationships? Findings from the New Family Structures Study," was published in the well-regarded professional journal *Social Science Research*.[55] Regnerus' research findings in this article suggested that adult children of parents who had had one or more same-sex romantic relationships fared significantly worse as adults on many emotional and material measures than their adult peers who were raised in an intact, biological family. Regnerus was clear in his article that his findings did not point in any specific policy direction[56]—in fact, his findings could have been just as plausibly interpreted as support for gay marriage as opposition to it, as I explain below.

Regnerus' survey data and measures were not without some problems—*something that is true of nearly every sociology article*

---

55. Volume 41, Issue 4, July 2012, pp. 752–770. Loren Marks also published an article in the same issue that essentially agreed with Regnerus' conclusions ("Same-Sex Parenting and Children's Outcomes: A Closer Examination of the American Psychological Association's Brief on Lesbian and Gay Parenting," pp. 735–751), which was criticized too, but not nearly as much as Regnerus' since it was essentially a literature review, not based on original research.

56. "Same-sex couples have and will continue to raise children," he wrote. "American courts are finding arguments against gay marriage decreasingly persuasive. *This study is intended to neither undermine nor affirm any legal rights concerning such*" (2012a: 766, italics added for emphasis). Four months later, Regnerus repeated: "Some perceive [my previous article] as a tool for this or that political project, a role it was never designed to fill. It *cannot answer political or legal questions*, and is by definition a retrospective look at household composition and dynamics" (2012b: 1367, italics added). In his write-up of his findings for *Slate*, Regnerus also stated this balanced view explicitly: "This study arrives in the middle of a season that's already exhibited plenty of high drama over same-sex marriage. . . . *The political take-home message of the NFSS study is unclear, however*," nothing that "the instability detected *in the NFSS could translate into a call for extending the relative security afforded by marriage to gay and lesbian couples*" (Mark Regnerus, 2012, "Queers as Folk: Does it Really Make no Difference if your Parents are Straight or Gay?" [the article title was written by *Slate*, not Regnerus], *Slate*, posted Monday, June 11, 2012, italics added).

published—yet his methods and sample were superior to any similar study on the topic conducted previously.[57] His article, when actually read (which many involved do not seem to have done), also includes all of the necessary and standard caveats, cautions, and recognitions of its limitations.[58] In truth, in an area of research (the comparative effects of same-sex parenting[59]) that had until then (and even in a few other studies since then) been conducted using very weak samples, Regnerus' study was the (relatively) best study conducted to date, the state of the art at the time, so to

57. For example, Henny Bos, Frank van Balen, and Dymphna van den Boom, 2007, "Child Adjustment and Parenting in Planned Lesbian Parent Families," *American Journal of Orthopsychiatry*, 77: 38–48; Anne Brewaeys, Ingrid Ponjaert, Eylard Van Hall, and Susan Golombok, 1997, "Donor Insemination: Child Development and Family Functioning in Lesbian Mother Families," *Human Reproduction*, 12: 1349–1359; Megan Fulcher, Erin Sutfin, and Charlotte Patterson, 2008, "Individual Differences in Gender Development: Associations with Parental Sexual Orientation, Attitudes, and Division of Labor," *Sex Roles*, 57: 330–341; Theodora Sirota, 2009, "Adult Attachment Style Dimensions in Women who have Gay or Bisexual Fathers," *Archives of Psychiatric Nursing*, 23: 289–297; Katrien Vanfraussen, Ingrid Ponjaert-Kristoffersen, and Anne Brewaeys, 2003, "Family Functioning in Lesbian Families Created by Donor Insemination," *American Journal of Orthopsychiatry*, 73: 78–90, which typically used snowball and convenience sampling methods.

58. He could not have been clearer: "There are several things the NFSS is not. The NFSS is not a longitudinal study, and therefore cannot attempt to broach questions of causation. It is a cross-sectional study, and collected data from respondents at only one point in time, when they were between the ages of 18 and 39. *It does not evaluate the offspring of gay marriages, since the vast majority of its respondents came of age prior to the legalization of gay marriage in several states. This study cannot answer political questions about same-sex relationships and their legal legitimacy*" (2012: 775). "To be sure, those NFSS respondents who reported that a parent of theirs had had a romantic relationship with a member of the same sex are a very diverse group: some experienced numerous household transitions, and some did not. Some of their parents may have remained in a same-sex relationship, while others did not. Some may self-identify as lesbian or gay, while others may not. I did not explore in detail the diversity of household experiences here" (2012: 765). "I have not and will not speculate here on causality, in part because the data are not optimally designed to do so. . . . I am thus not suggesting that growing up with a lesbian mother or gay father causes suboptimal outcomes because of the sexual orientation or sexual behavior of the parent; rather, my point is more modest: the groups display numerous, notable distinctions, especially when compared with young adults whose biological mother and father remain married" (2012: 766).

59. Or, more pertinent to Regnerus' study, having a parent who had same-sex relationships.

THE SACRED PROJECT OF AMERICAN SOCIOLOGY

speak, even if the state of the art was (and still is) not impressive.[60] In a response to Regnerus' article in the same issue, Paul Amato, then chair of the Family section of the ASA and president-elect of the National Council on Family Relations, wrote that the Regnerus study was "better situated than virtually all previous studies to detect differences between these [different family] groups in the population."[61] Important to know is that *sociologists had never criticized any of the methodologically very weak studies published before Regnerus' article* on this topic. Why? Because those studies had concluded that same-sex parenting had no negative effects on children. Since those weak studies produced the "right" findings for sociology's sacred project, nobody in the discipline was concerned to critique their serious, at times pathetically bad, methodological flaws.

Regnerus' article, however, came to a different conclusion, one that was heretical and blasphemous to sociology's sacred project. So it provoked, in contrast to the acceptance of previous publications, an absolute firestorm of reaction. The denunciations, criticisms, and professional dissociations were emotional and exaggerated beyond reason, completely flaming, truly over the top. "Breathtakingly sloppy," "pseudo-science," and "gets everything wrong"[62]

---

60. Regnerus' findings related to instability, also note, are consistent with recent studies of gay and lesbian couples based on large, random, representative samples from countries such as Great Britain, the Netherlands, and Sweden, which find similarly high patterns of instability among same-sex couples (Gunnar Andersson et al., 2006, "The Demographics of Same-Sex Marriages in Norway and Sweden," *Demography*, 43: 79–98; Matthijs Kalmijn et al., 2007, "Income Dynamics in Couples and the Dissolution of Marriage and Cohabitation," *Demography*, 44: 159–179; Charles Strohm, 2010, "The Formation and Stability of Same-Sex and Different-Sex Relationships," University of California Sociology Department Dissertation, Los Angeles).

61. Amato, 2012, "The Well-being of Children with Gay and Lesbian Parents," *Social Science Research*, 41: 735–751.

62. Amy Davidson, "A Faulty 'Gay Parenting' Study," *The New Yorker*, June 12, 2012; John Corvino, "Are Gay Parents Really Worse for Children? How a New Study Gets Everything Wrong," *The New Republic,* June 11, 2012.

were among the early descriptors of his article.[63] To any genuinely fair-minded person who has actually read Regnerus' article, it is

63. As a matter of fact—and *this is absolutely crucial to grasp*—the differences in findings (whether children of same-sex couples fare worse or whether there is "no difference") in all such articles are finally determined by whether or not their statistical models do or do not control for a "household stability" variable. Regnerus' did not do so for arguably good theoretical and analytic reasons, and found what he found; other studies that do control for stability inevitably find "no difference." Had Regnerus also controlled for household stability, he would in fact have found "no difference" and become the darling of the activists who ended up assaulting him. Much of the controversy thus comes down to this "lies, damned lies, and statistics" problem. Sociologists who want to find "no difference" can control for household stability and arrive at their desired findings. The debate thus largely hinges upon the *conceptual* question of whether "household stability" should be treated as a *statistical control* versus explaining *the causal mechanism* by which children with same-sex parents come to exhibit statistically significantly different (negative) life outcomes.

Here then is the bottom line of what's going on: Same-sex households on average have had higher levels of instability than heterosexual households (whether this remains true in the future we do not know), and such instability causes greater problems in the lives of children who come from them. We know this. Yet *instability does not cause same-sex households*, rather the opposite: some features about same-sex relationships in our society (that last point about society context being potentially decisive) produce experiences of greater household instability. Sociologists advocating the "no difference" conclusion argue that it is *really* the instability per se, not the same-sex feature, of the household that produces the worse outcome results. That turns "instability" into a generic variable abstracted away from the causally driven disproportionate amount of instability that in fact characterizes same-sex households. However, if that instability is actually caused by something about the same-sex nature of the parent relationships (in the context of a certain kind of society and culture), then controlling for instability only obscures our understanding of how and why the mechanisms-process works to produce outcomes. Otherwise, one would have to claim that the same-sex factor is spurious, which does not make sense. (Consider, for example, another study—Daniel Potter, 2012, "Same-Sex Parent Families and Children's Academic Achievement," *Journal of Marriage and Family*, 74: 556–571—which also, like Regnerus', was based on a large, nationally representative sample, and which found that "children in same-sex parent families scored lower than their peers in married, 2-biological parent households" on academic outcomes, arguing that these baseline differences can probably be attributed in part to higher levels of family instability in same-sex families, compared to intact, biological married families.)

Instead, by running statistical models with household stability removed, one can first demonstrate what appears to be the link between same-sex households and worse outcomes for children. That is what Regnerus did in his article. Then, by running more models with instability included, when the same-sex variable becomes insignificant, one thus demonstrates that *instability is the causal mechanism* by which same-sex parent clear that the vast majority of its critics had not actually personally read it, or do not understand enough about social science to make an informed judgment about it—which is why many in fact failed to make a reasonable judgment about it. Regnerus' study was also charged with being inevitably biased because it was funded by a conservative organization[64], which demonstrated a pure hypocrisy of flagrant double standards, since other related studies that were not similarly criticized had been funded by very "interested" groups, including numerous LGBT organizations[65] (which funded

environments (again, measures in the past) produce those worse outcomes for children. That kind of logic and analysis is of course used and conducted all the time in sociology with "nested models" regression. The "problem" in this case, however, is that treating household instability as a mediating causal mechanism rather than a control variable reveals what appears to be the fact of statistically significantly worse outcomes for children with same-sex pa`rents—which is politically unacceptable. So the standard practice on this research question has become to always *control* for household instability and thus make the unacceptable finding of worse outcomes go away. But that is like showing (as a hypothetical example) that attending public schools in richer neighborhoods does not really cause more access to admissions to "better" colleges because if one controls for student SAT scores and impressiveness of résumés and application essays, then neighborhood wealth and school resources become statistically insignificant—which, any sociologist would know, is ridiculous. But apparently anything now that deviates from the currently standard approach—even if for better analytic reasons—is now defined as "breathtakingly sloppy" and "gets everything wrong."

Finally, as I say below, one could very well accept Regnerus' analysis, argue very plausibly that the greater instability of same-sex households measured to date is not inevitable but is due to the lack of institutional support and the cultural stigma that is attached to them, and claim on that basis that the outcomes of children raised in same-sex households could be significantly improved by increasing institutional recognition and support and removing that stigma, by accepting legal same-sex marriages. That alternative interpretation is just as plausible, if not more so, as the one most used to attack Regnerus.

64. http://winst.org/.

65. Including the Arcus Foundation (which "works to advance LGBT equality," http://www.arcusfoundation.org/), the Gill Foundation ("advocates for LGBT equality," http://gillfoundation.org/), the Lesbian Health Fund of the Gay and Lesbian Medical Association, the Roy Scrivner Fund of the American Psychological Association (which "encourages the study of lesbian, gay, bisexual and transgender (LGBT) family psychology and LGBT family therapy," http://www.apa.org/apf/funding/scrivner.aspx), and the Uncommon Legacy Foundation, which supports lesbian students—see http://www.nllfs.org/about/supporters/.

the National Longitudinal Lesbian Family Study) and Church & Dwight Co., the manufacturer of Trojan condoms (which funded the Indiana University National Survey of Sexual Health and Behavior study on sexual health). Nevertheless, outraged groups of sociologists teamed up with gay-rights political activists, gay-rights "journalists," and non-sociology faculty-supporters of sociology's sacred mission from other disciplines to discredit Regnerus' article, to smear his scholarly reputation, and to persecute him legally and institutionally.[66] It was pure politicized science, as Richard Redding later pointed out, involving massive amounts of "sociopolitical groupthink."[67] What unfolded, as I pointed out at the time in an editorial in the *Chronicle of Higher Education*, was a genuine, modern-day academic Inquisition and political witch trial.[68] The editor of *Social Science Research* was also severely questioned and condemned for simply having published the article. The review process by which the article had been unanimously judged worthy of publication by six double-blind reviewers was subject to a special investigation by one of sociology's spiritual project's most active advocates.[69] And

66. One particularly aggressive gay-rights "journalist"—who operated like a thug and character assassin—pressed the University of Texas at Austin administration into conducting a scientific-misconduct inquiry about Regnerus (which he immediately [mis] labeled in his articles "an investigation," which, however, of course eventually exonerated Regnerus); used Freedom of Information Act requests to make public Regnerus' university emails related to his research; and harassed and attempted to intimidate those scholars (including yours truly), who were not so intimidated by the hysterical witch hunt that they were willing to attempt to publicly defend Regnerus on the merits of his study, by contacting their department chairs and university's administrative and communications officers with "urgent" ("fishing expedition") accusatory emails, requests for ethics inquiries, charges of lying, and demands to have their email records made public.

67. Richard Redding, 2013, "Politicized Science," *Society*, August, 50(5): 439–446.

68. Christian Smith, 2012, "An Academic Auto-da-Fé," *The Chronicle of Higher Education*, Opinion & Ideas section, July 23.

69. See Gary J. Gates et al., 2012, "Letter to the Editors and Advisory Editors of Social Science Research," *Social Science Research*, 41: 1350–1351. For the journal editor's response and explanation of the affair from his perspective, which essentially vindicated Regnerus, see James Wright, 2012, "Introductory Remarks," *Social Science Research*, 41:

the reputable professional survey firm that collected Regnerus' data was slandered.[70] The resulting academic and national media pandemonium turned Regnerus into a political lightning rod in sociology and gay-rights activist circles during the summer of 2012 and throughout the following fall. For his part, Regnerus mostly stayed above the fray, made his dataset public on October 2, and published a smart and convincing (I think) response to his critics in November 2012.[71] Regnerus' study and the controversy that

1339–1345. Also, an LGBT activist, "independent journalist," and blogger has filed a public records lawsuit against the University of Central Florida's Board of Trustees and President, seeking access to records relating to the journal's publication of Regnerus, which, if successful, would disclose, among other things, the identities and correspondence of the six peer reviewers of Regnerus' paper (http://knightnews.com/2013/04/activist-files-public-records-lawsuit-against-ucf-trustees-hitt/). In late June 2013, the University of Central Florida was said to have released 15,000 emails to plaintiffs investigating the review of the paper, accidentally also including private emails of students protected by FERPA privacy laws (http://knightnews.com/2013/06/ucf-admits-to-releasing-private-student-records-in-lawsuit-video/).

70. Even though it is the same survey firm that collected the data for that year's National Science Foundation-funded American National Election Survey (the political science equivalent of sociology's General Social Survey); the Indiana University National Survey of Sexual Health and Behavior study on sexual health (funded by condom manufacturing companies noted on p. 107), the findings of which were reported in an entire issue of the *Journal of Sexual Medicine*; as well as data for many other publications in top sociology journals, including one in *ASR* (Michael Rosenfeld and Reuben Thomas, 2012, "Searching for a Mate: the Rise of the Internet as a Social Intermediary," *American Sociological Review*, 77: 523–547), by the same scholar, incidentally, who elsewhere published an article similar to Regnerus' (Michael Rosenfeld, 2010, "Nontraditional Families and Childhood Progress through School," *Demography*, 47: 755–775) but that came to different conclusions, largely because he controlled for family stability and Regnerus did not (see footnote 63); see Douglas Allen, Catherine Pakaluk, and Joseph Price, 2012, "Nontraditional Families and Childhood Progress Through School: A Comment on Rosenfeld," *Demography*, 50: 955–961, which replicated Rosenfeld's study using alternative (arguably better) comparison groups and alternative sample restrictions and concluded, "Compared with traditional married households, we find that children being raised by same-sex couples are 35 percent less likely to make normal progress through school; this difference is statistically significant at the 1 percent level."

71. Mark Regnerus, 2012, "Parental Same-Sex Relationships, Family Instability, and Subsequent Life Outcomes for Adult Children: Answering Critics of the New Family Structures Study with Additional Analyses," *Social Science Research*, 41: 1367–1377— which of course his hysterical critics largely ignored, having already by then done most of the damage they could.

followed it eventually played a significant role in the *amicus* brief filed by the ASA with the U.S. Supreme Court in February 2013, which went to great pains explicitly to dismiss Regnerus' research and instead to present other research producing different ("correct") findings as representing the most reliable evidence to which the Justices should pay attention in their judicial considerations, the ASA hoping thereby to help prompt the Court on empirical grounds to strike down (which it eventually did) Section 3 of the Defense of Marriage Act, the constitutionality of which the Court had agreed to review, and to not overturn a lower trial court's decision denying the "standing" of challenges to California's Proposition 8's constitutionality.[72] The repercussions of this debacle reverberate down to even the time of this writing. GLBTQ activist "journalists" continue to use judicial means, with some success, to force the journal *Social Science Research* and the University of Central Florida, where its editor works, to turn over hundreds of email documents that would disclose the personal identities of journal reviewers and student workers to be posted on the Internet, most of which has nothing to do with the review of the Regnerus paper.[73]

---

72. ASA, 2013, "Speaking for Science: ASA Submits an Amicus Brief to the U.S. Supreme Court," *Footnotes*, 41(3): 2. Another *amicus* brief was also filed by another group of scholars that both included references to Regnerus' work and was joined by Regnerus himself.

73. On one example of activists' legal intrusions into the blind peer-review process of scholarship: http://miamiherald.typepad.com/gaysouthflorida/2013/11/hrc-florida-judge-orders-university-to-turn-over-records-from-study-used-to-demonize-gay-parents.html. In this lawsuit, a GBLTQ "journalist" sued the University of Central Florida (UCF) for hundreds of email correspondences between the journal *Social Science Research*'s editor and many people involved (and not involved) in the review of the Regnerus paper. UCF initially honored a first request for emails by releasing many thousands of them. Subsequently, UCF requested that hundreds of those records be redacted to protect unrelated personal information before being posted on the activist's website (http://knightnews.com/2013/06/ucf-admits-to-releasing-private-student-records-in-lawsuit-video/). That request was refused. UCF also claimed that

Amid the still-clearing smoke, it is imperative to focus on the most crucial fact. The important point about this entire debacle concerned *not* the details of Regnerus' sample, survey questions, data coding, statistical analyses, or substantive conclusions—all of which were much debated and denounced as the issues that his critics wished to highlight.[74] Instead, the most important fact about this travesty of sociological justice—which, no matter how obvious it was and is, most sociologists I communicated with could never see, admit, or consider—was the *blatant double standard of methodological and political criticism very selectively condemning Regnerus but never applied to any other scholarly research publication on the same topic despite their typically relying on much weaker samples and analytic methods.* Any reasonably open-minded comparison by

the release of these 357 records was inadvertent and ill advised, since not only was students' personal information included but, UCF alleged, the emails actually belong not to UCF but to the publisher of *Social Science Research.* Also, while activists repeatedly characterize the records as those "related to the Regnerus study," most of them in fact have nothing to do with it, but are about editor Jim Wright's own research on marriage, suggesting the motive to harass more than to uncover genuinely illegitimate review processes. Support for action against editor Wright is driven by a small number of activists, as evidenced by the main petition for it that had accumulated only 141 signatures in two months: http://www.change.org/petitions/ucf-provost-tony-waldrop-discipline-regnerus-editor-james-wright-2. The most recent ruling of Orange County Circuit Court Judge Donald Grincewicz as of this writing stated that the 357 records need not be redacted and that UCF must turn over additional records requested. UCF has not complied as of this writing. Judge Grincewicz has also since apparently recused himself from the case. The bottom line is that if scholars working for a public institution publish a piece of scholarship that is viewed by some as unfavorable to the cause of same-sex marriage and GLBTQ rights, their emails, professional history, and personal information regarding their students and colleagues are vulnerable to being forced into public exposure; and any other scholars who serve as blind peer reviewers of such a paper for possible publication are subject to having their confidential status stripped away and their communications made public on the Internet. As of this writing, no evidence suggests that the ASA intends to take a principled stand on the matter in defense of the journal editor and peer reviewers. Also see http://regnerusfallout.org/.

74. Regnerus parsed the various critiques carefully and responds to them well in his 2012b paper; also see a thorough summary in Wood, 2013, pp. 174–176; also see Redding, 2013, pp. 441–442.

any even moderately perceptive person could see that *the only dif-ference explaining why Regnerus and his article were assaulted and the other publications and their authors were never attacked is that Regnerus' study produced the "wrong" findings and the previous stud-ies produced the "correct" findings.* No other difference explains the gross discrepancy in critical response from so many sociologists.[75] The real problem was not that it was a particularly bad article sci-entifically, but that it was a "politically insensitive article," in the frank and revealing words of a sociologist commentator who wrote in a subsequent issue of the same journal.[76] Those very few of us who pointed out this uncomfortable fact at the time were brushed aside or ignored. (My argument all along was that the negative re-action against Regnerus was stupid, even for gay-rights activists, since his findings lend themselves just as well to arguments sup-porting legal gay marriage as opposing it.[77] But the nerve that was

75. In a follow-up evaluation of Regnerus' article, the Kansas State University sociolo-gist Walter Schumm correctly stated this: "Every social science researcher must make a number of methodological decisions when planning and implementing research projects. Each such decision carries with it both advantages and limitations. . . . . Even though the apparent outcomes of Regnerus's study were unpopular, *the methodological decisions he made in the design and implementation of the New Family Structures Survey were not uncommon among social scientists, including many progressive, gay and lesbian scholars. These decisions and the research they produced deserve considerable and continued discussion, but criticisms of the underlying ethics and professionalism are misplaced because nearly every methodological decision that was made has ample precedents in research pub-lished by many other credible and distinguished scholars"* (Schumm, 2012, "Methodologi-cal Decisions and the Evaluation of Possible Effects of Different Family Structures on Children: The New Family Structures Survey," *Social Science Research*, 41: 1357–1366, italics added for emphasis).
76. Don Barrett, 2012, "Presentation, Politics, and Editing: The Marks/Regnerus Arti-cles," *Social Science Research*, 41(6): 771–774—the telling phrase is found on p. 3, where Barrett asks, "so my immediate question was how could he [the editor] have published such problematic and *politically insensitive articles?"*
77. Specifically, since Regnerus' adult sample would have encountered their parental expe-rience with a same-sex relationship decades earlier as children, when same-sex relation-ships were viewed as far more socially deviant, and since that very culturally defined deviance was certainly part (if not all) of what produced the findings that children of such parents suffered significantly more emotional and psychological difficulties as

touched was apparently too sensitive for that kind of cleverness.) Some sociologists whom I personally pressed hard on their obvious double standard and inquisitional persecution of Regnerus ended up finally telling me, "Well, *what do you expect us to do* when something this so politically important comes out at a time like this?"[78] In short, they frankly conceded that I was right about the double standard, but asserted that it was justified and necessary, given the political climate and Regnerus' "political insensitivity." Some who took that view added that Regnerus deserved exactly what he got, even if he had been singled out for formal investigation, media smearing, and denunciation by his colleagues.[79] Nor

adults, it is easy to interpret those findings as (further) justifying the need to finally eliminate the labeling of same-sex relationships as deviant, by legalizing gay marriage. That embrace and interpretation of the findings would have been easy and completely plausible.

78. The larger political context was not irrelevant to what played out: The article was "coincidentally published a few months after President Obama's May 2012 White House interview with Robin Roberts of ABC News in which he endorsed same-sex marriage. And it appeared in the midst of what the *New York Times*, in a review of *Victory: The Triumph of the Gay Revolution*, called 'Banner Days.' Former stalwart opponents of same-sex marriage such as Institute for American Values David Blankenhorn had just announced their change of heart. National polls were showing dramatic swings of public opinion in favor of legalized gay marriage, and the issue was headed to the U.S. Supreme Court. Democrat and Republican senators and congressmen who had been adamantly opposed to same-sex marriage were discovering new convictions contrary to their previous views. By almost any reckoning, advocates of same-sex marriage had the cultural winds at their back. In this context, Regnerus' article stood out as a relative isolate." Peter Wood, 2013, "The Campaign to Discredit Regnerus and the Assault on Peer Review," *Academic Questions*, 26: 171–181, quoted from p. 171.

79. One version of this sentiment was that Regnerus "crossed a line" by publishing a popular press article about his findings in *Slate*. While I think he would have been prudent not to have written the *Slate* article, the fact is that sociologists do such things *all the time* and it is considered great to get "sociology in the news." The ASA even invites journalists to come to its annual meetings and cover research presented, and every issue of the ASA's monthly members' newsletter, *Footnotes*, includes a "Sociologists in the News" section. So justifying the assault on Regnerus on the grounds that he wrote a popular press article on his findings is hypocritical. (In fact, literally 30 minutes after having just worked on this section, I received two emails from the ASA's Media Relations and Public Affairs Officer, seeking to recruit sociologists to speak with journalists, saying this: "The ASA is continuing to expand its database of ASA members who

was the matter forgotten. During the spring of 2013, for instance, one of Regnerus' senior colleagues from UT-Austin was reported by credible sources to be giving professional talks as a visiting speaker to faculty and graduate students at other sociology departments, in which she was referencing the controversy and publicly referring to Regnerus as "He Who Must Not Be Named"—that is, the hideously evil and malevolent Lord Voldemort from the popular J. R. Rowling *Harry Potter* book and movie series. Amazing it will be, in this kind of context, if Regnerus is ever promoted to the rank of Full Professor, no matter how objectively deserving of promotion he may in due time be.[80]

Long story short: Mark Regnerus dared to publish peer-reviewed sociological findings that cut the sacred project of American sociology to the quick, and consequently he was made, no matter how unjustly, irrationally, or indefensibly, to pay a personally and professionally highly damaging price for doing so. Also very important is this fact: As collateral damage in social science more broadly, *the chance that any other sociologist will publish findings similar to Regnerus' or even consider researching this topic with an open mind, that any sociology journal editor will consider publishing another article like his no matter how solid the data and analyses, or that any potential journal-article reviewer will ever even consider accepting the job of reviewing such an article at the request of any editor has been reduced to zilch* by the way that Regnerus was put on public sham trial and damned.

are subject matter experts and who are willing to talk with reporters. This database serves as an easily accessible resource that ASA Public Affairs and Public Information (PA/PI) staff consult when journalists request interviews with experts for their stories.")

80. Ridiculous Internet stories also continue to surface, keeping the controversy alive, such as the laughably embellished and false, "Explosive Documents Reveal Sham Regnerus 'Study' Was Rigged from the Start." John M. Becker (blog), March 11, 2013, http://www.johnmbecker.com/2013/03/11/sham-regnerus-study-was-rigged-from-the-start/.

Now, I want to be absolutely clear about my point in telling these anecdotes above. I am not suggesting that these kinds of things are normal in everyday sociology. Such things have happened and do happen in sociology and beyond. But I am not saying that sociology is a fraudulent and corrupt discipline full of crooked characters and shady dealers, or rampant with unprincipled, self-interested activists seeking to deceive their opponents and the public. My point, in fact, is in some ways nearly the opposite: American sociology as an academic discipline is possessed by a powerful, "righteous," sacred vision that forcefully defines its moral, ideological, and political activities in ways that give sociology real energy, focus, and vitality—for better, at times, and for worse, at others. Sociology is on a mission to actively promote an ultimate vision of (what it believes to be) the true good, the highest meaning, the ultimate values, the very best for human living—and woe to the one who gets in the way. Most of the individual sociologists who get caught up in this dynamic are not bad people, either, any more than you or I are—most (but certainly not all) in fact are quite decent and well-meaning. And in all of this, sociology transcends mere scientific, material, and utilitarian interests. What is at stake here far surpasses the mundane issues of mere organizational power or the protection of institutional territory or resources. American sociology is, much more profoundly and at its heart, deeply *spiritually committed*, engaged in the veneration and promotion of a Durkheimian sacred. Most of the anecdotes recounted above are not "typical" of sociology in the sense of everyday experience. But they do reveal some of the ways that American sociology's sacred project is expressed in specific instances and some of the odd difficulties and even gross injustices it can provoke and produce.

Chapter 3

Spiritual Practices

No spirituality consists only of ideas, visions, and values. Spiritualties always involve self- and world-transforming *practices* as well. To pursue a spiritual project requires engaging in disciplined behaviors that shape the self and perhaps the surrounding world to conform to the spiritual ideas, visions, and values in question. Monks and saints do this. So do American sociologists, in their own way. What, then, are the transformative disciplines and practices of American sociology's sacred project? They are something like the following, which we might think of as "Sociology's 12 Steps to Spiritual Enlightenment and Growth":

Step 1: Undertake a long apprenticeship of demanding training in graduate school to learn the right ways of seeing the ultimate truth about reality, to learn to transcend ordinary understandings of lay men and women, to correctly re-describe the world of appearances in the approved worldview, and to pass the tests of discipline that finally admit one as an approved disciple into the fold of the enlightened ones.

Step 2: Never cease to read, think, and talk about the Masters— Marx, Durkheim, Weber, Goffman, Berger, and Bourdieu (advanced disciples move up to Foucault, the esoteric Judith Butler, etcetera)—and to apply them to all aspects of life, continually refining one's ability to divine between reality and illusion.

Step 3: Rummage throughout the mess of human society and find a good outrage, an injustice, a slight, an oppression, about which one feels especially affronted and others should too, that needs to be exposed as a social problem demanding retributive destruction as a redemptive and cathartic sacrifice paying the just price to achieve humanity's salvation.

Step 4: Through an arduous program of research, writing, teaching, attending meetings, presenting papers, writing and publishing articles and books, and traveling the land to speak and listen, tell near and far the bad news of the power of society's evils that must be overcome and the good news of the promise of salvation through personal conversion, social transformation, and the eventual collective realization of justice, equality, and mutual affirmation.

Step 5: Learn the magic of summoning "science" to prevent fully revealing to the uninitiated the entire breadth and depth of the sacred vision, the doctrines of the sacred gnosis, and the dream of the liberated world to come; then master the subtler art of suspending from one's own consciousness the higher truths that animate one's sacred community— through the constant hum of computer statistics programs crunching numbers, if necessary.

Step 6: Recruit new convert neophytes to the sacred project from among the most promising young students, identifying those who are truly called by the sign of their ineffable experience of "getting it" after only introductory instruction, an experience of enlightenment they will most assuredly share with you after class or during office hours.

Step 7: Regularly attend regional and national gatherings of faithful believers and practitioners to share with them your own personal advances of growth in the sacred project, to recite together the project's mantras, and to reinforce the project's necessary plausibility structures sustaining your shared beliefs and commitments.

Step 8: Prove one's worthiness after the appointed years by undergoing and passing the tests of review and promotion, winning the testimony of greater masters concerning one's unique contribution to the shared, disciplined, sacred project.

Step 9: Meet regularly over cappuccinos and biscotti in cells and cliques, and over papers and PowerPoint presentations in workshops and colloquia, to meditate on evils in the social world and to recite together the doctrinal truths and prefiguring experiences of its redemption.

Step 10: Discipline oneself to remove from one's mind all unhelpful thoughts (that might threaten to demand a big transformation of one's own lifestyle) about the radical disjuncture between the nice life that most academic disciples of the sacred project enjoy and those lived by the truly poor, oppressed, exploited, deprived, and dying souls whose lives the project will one day liberate—it is truly more blessed to talk about them in the New York Hilton than to know and serve them directly in one's own life.[1]

Step 11: If one becomes genuinely worthy, ascend to the rank of Great Master of the sacred project, helping to lead other,

1. A telling anecdote: The 2013 ASA Annual Meeting materials provided to registered participants included a booklet entitled "The Corpulent Social Scientist's Guide to New York City Dining" (the meeting's theme was "Interrogating Inequality").

lesser disciples into higher levels of conscientization, critical analysis, and career success.

Step 12: Remain alert and ever vigilant against false sheep, heretics, and traitors within the fold who threaten to betray the project, and against wolves, philistines, and conservatives outside of the fold who threaten to cut the project's funding—be prepared if dire need arises to sacrifice one's own standards of reason and fairness to eliminate the former and obstruct the latter.

In truth, if one is not prepared to turn one's back on the distractions and temptations that would prevent one from putting these spiritual practices into action, one is not fit for sociology's project.

Chapter 4

How Did We Get Here?— The Short Story

American sociologists misunderstand and pay little attention to their own deep history and its meaning, at the price of ignorance and lack of self-understanding. That is ironic for a discipline that insists on telling others how much there is to learn at the "intersection of biography and history," using the fertile phrase of the radical sociologist C. Wright Mills.[1] To properly understand contemporary American sociology's sacred project, we need to place it in some historical context, even one very briefly set out, as I do here.

The sacred project I have described is not a recent development. Some of its particular features today are recent accretions, but all of it is built on the momentum of a much longer disciplinary project. Sociology is an archetypically modern endeavor, and its deepest spiritual roots are sunk in the soil of the early modern era, particularly in the modern project of reconstituting society on

1. Mills, 1959, *The Sociological Imagination*, New York: Grove Press.

a rational, universal, secular basis. With the demise of Christendom and the rise of wars of early modern regional political territories and nation-states that often involved religious conflicts—that were later labeled "religious wars"[2]—European thinkers became increasingly convinced of the need to ground social orders not on shared religious commitments (as in European Christendom) but on a more secular basis that would provide greater social stability and material prosperity.[3] Understood this way, modernity was about taking human destiny out of the sovereign hands of God and from the fixed determination of a cosmic natural order, and instead placing human destiny in the hands of a willful, autonomous, self-determining humanity. James Faubian, following the view of Max Weber, correctly observes:

> The existential threshold of modernity [is found] in a certain deconstruction: of what [Max Weber] speaks of as the "ethical postulate that the world is God-ordained". . . . The threshold of modernity may be marked precisely at the moment when the unquestioned legitimacy of a divinely preordained social order began to decline. Modernity emerges . . . only when what has been seen as an unchanging cosmos ceases to be taken for granted.[4]

2. In fact, modern people badly misunderstand the nature of the so-called "Wars of Religion," in ways that serve the purpose of secular liberalism. See William Cavanaugh's excellent *The Myth of Religious Violence: Secular Ideology and the Roots of Modern Conflict* (New York: Oxford University Press, 2009).

3. Brad Gregory, 2012, *The Unintended Reformation: How a Religious Revolution Secularized Society*, Cambridge: Harvard University Press. For an analysis of modern Western secularism's highly particular views of human agency and authority, particularly its connection to the "romance of resistance" that is central to American sociology, see Talal Asad, 2003, *Formations of the Secular: Christianity, Islam, Modernity*, Stanford: Stanford University Press.

4. Faubion, 1993, *Modern Greek Lessons: A Primer in Historical Constuctivism*, Princeton: Princeton University Press, quoted in Eisenstadt, 2000, p. 4.

Following this idea, Shmuel Eisenstadt rightly states this:

> Central to [the modern] cultural program was an emphasis
> on the autonomy of man: his or her . . . emancipation from
> the fetters of traditional political and cultural authority. From
> [this] . . . arose a belief in the possibility that society could be
> actively formed by conscious human activity. . . . Central to the
> modern idea was the breakdown of all traditional legitimations
> of the political order, and with it the opening up of different
> possibilities in the construction of a new order.[5]

Once this larger program of modernity started to gain serious momentum in the early nineteenth century, "Sociology" was invented as the new "science of society" and authorized to provide modernity's vanguard the scientific tools by which to understand, explain, control, and reconstruct human societies.[6] Sociology was necessary for the building of modernity's new social order of freedom from both oppressive social restrictions (through emancipation and perhaps revolution) and material constraints (through the material prosperity produced by humanity's mastery of nature). Out of the deepest core of modernity, therefore, drive the dual impulses of freedom and control, of autonomy and mastery, of emancipation

---

5. S. N. Eistenstadt, 2000, "Multiple Modernities," *Daedalus*, pp. 3–5. Eisenstadt continues: "The cultural and political program of modernity . . . entailed some very distinct shifts in the conception of human agency, and of its place in the flow of time. It carried the conception of the future characterized by a number of possibilities realizable through autonomous human agency. The premises on which the social, ontological, and political order were based, and the legitimation of that order, were no longer taken for granted. An intensive reflexivity developed around the basic ontological premises of structures of social and political authority. . . . The modern program . . . came to question the very givenness of such visions [of pre-modern, 'axial' civilizations] and the institutional patterns related to them" (pp. 3–5).
6. Smith, 2003, pp. 97–159.

and discipline.[7] Sociology's unique historical task in all of this has been to apply the scientific method to "society" in order to produce the scientific knowledge needed for modernity's vanguard to exert the social control and mastery necessary to construct emancipatory societies granting individuals maximum freedom and autonomy. The fact that human freedom, autonomy, and emancipation stand in tension with social control, mastery, and discipline is obvious, but this tension is precisely what gives modernity its dynamic energy and uneasiness.[8] It also provides sociology with some of its internal strains and instabilities.

Returning to our main theme, we can see a sacred character already infusing sociology from its founding. As a project, sociology belonged at the heart of a movement that self-consciously and intentionally displaced western Christianity's integrative and directive role in society. It was a key partner in modernity's world-historical efforts to create a secular, rational, scientific social order. In this sense, sociology as a discipline operated *functionally* in direct *structural parallel* to the Roman Catholic Vatican's Curia and European Protestantism's early modern theology faculty—all being assigned the task of conducting the systematic intellectual work undergirding attempts to exert far-reaching influence over society. Sociology was not merely about piecemeal reforms but *world transformation guided by a radically new sacred vision of humanity, life, society, and the cosmos.*[9]

Early American sociologist pioneers and textbook authors— such as Lester Ward, Albion Small, Franklin Giddings, George

7. Eisenstadt, 2000, pp. 7–8; Peter Wagner, 1993, *A Sociology of Modernity: Freedom and Discipline*, London: Routledge.
8. Leszek Kolakowski, 1990, *Modernity on Endless Trial*, Chicago: University of Chicago Press.
9. See Thomas Haskell, 1977, *The Emergence of Professional Social Science*, Urbana: University of Illinois Press; Ross, 1991; Mary Furner, 1975, *Advocacy and Objectivity*, Lexington: University Press of Kentucky; Robert Bruce, 1987, *The Launching of Modern American Science*, Ithaca, NY: Cornell University Press.

Vincent, Edward Ross, and James Dealey, among others—saw themselves engaged in exactly this kind of project. Early American sociologists actively pursued the double-minded task of seeking to legitimate sociology by appealing to its salvific and other alleged religion-like qualities, even while intentionally secularizing sociology and higher education generally by purging it of religious interlopers.[10] In due time, advocates of the Social Gospel and Christian socialism were pushed out of the academic discipline of sociology, yet sociology faculty took on the responsibility for many parallel roles formerly played by religion. In such subtle, multileveled ways, American sociology sustained a sacred vision, mission, and character—even if not always as self-reflexively as one might have hoped. To illustrate this, I present the following quotes from the most popular early sociology textbooks by some of its then-foremost thinkers.

In 1898, Lester Ward wrote that "The laws of nature have always proved capable of being turned to man's advantage . . . and there is no reason to suppose that those of human nature and of society will form an exception."[11] Eight years later, Ward stated that "Applied sociology aims at the complete social transformation which will follow the assimilation of discovered [sociological] truth."[12] Albion Small and George Vincent promised that sociology would help complete human existence: "The justification of Sociology will be its contribution to knowledge and its aid toward realizing the conditions of complete human life."[13] According to James Dealey, impending sociological knowledge of "social laws" would bring progress and happiness to humanity: "Sociologists now assert with

10. Smith, 2003, pp. 97–159.
11. Ward, 1898, *Outlines of Sociology*, New York: Macmillan, p. 199.
12. Ward, 1906, *Applied Sociology*, New York: Arno Press, p. 85.
13. Albion Small and George Vincent, 1894, *An Introduction to the Study of Society*, New York: American Book, p. 373.

increasing emphasis that the time is not far distant when some of the fundamental laws and principles underlying social activity will be so well understood that civilization can begin to exterminate the great handicaps to progress . . . and to build up with scientific precision a social order that will bring vigor and happiness to mankind."[14] As late as the mid-1920s, Edward Ross proclaimed that sociology provides, again, a highly modern tool of human *control* toward realizing human *desires*: "Why is it not legitimate to sound social phenomena in hopes of discovering how they may be controlled to suit our wishes? . . . Indeed, attack upon the maladjustments among men is an inevitable consequence of the development of social science."[15]

Oftentimes, the true sacred nature of sociology—as I have described that above—shone forth explicitly from these early American sociologists' textbooks. James Dealey, for instance, likened sociological insight to a kind of religious experience that provides inspiration for life because of its purpose of perfecting humanity: "When sociology lends itself so readily to a sort of religious interpretation of social movements, it is not strange that many persons find in it a kind of inspiration for life. Back of statistics, the cold logic of science is the belief in the perfectibility of mankind."[16] According to Lester Ward, sociology's task was to achieve human happiness: "The problem of dynamic sociology is the organization of happiness."[17] That would be achieved, Ward argued, by sociology's scientific understanding of social mechanisms, which—in contrast to religious "exhortations"—would overcome evil: "Evil is merely the friction [in 'social energy'] which is to be overcome or at least minimized. This cannot be done by exhortation. It must be done

14. Dealey, 1909, *Sociology*, New York: D. Appleton, pp. 65–66.
15. Ross, 1925, *Principles of Sociology*, New York: Century, p. 545.
16. Dealey, 1909, pp. 503–504.
17. Ward, 1883, *Dynamic Sociology*, New York: D. Appleton, p. 156.

by perfecting the social mechanism."[18] Not surprisingly, then, more than two decades later, Edward Hayes proclaimed that sociology's immodest goal as a social science was none other than to take over the human task of moral reasoning: "Sociology aims at nothing less than the transfer of ethics from the domain of speculative philosophy [including religion] to the domain of objective science."[19] In the conclusion of his sociology textbook, James Dealey proclaimed a "call to salvation," declaring that:

> [Humanity] looks forward to a time when man will come into his kingdom; when misery, vice, and human discord shall have been outgrown, and peace, good will, and joyous emulation in achievement will prevail among men. In anticipation he feels himself to be part of a glorified humanity, since he also does his share in the world's work, and builds up, be it ever so little, the achievements and happiness of mankind. This joy in companionship with men, past, living, and future, is to him immortality, and when death comes, since he is also a true son of man, and like Moses has caught a glimpse of the promised land, he goes gladly.[20]

These are spiritual writings, undeniably. American sociology was founded not simply as an objective, value-free, disinterested science of society: It was from the start a sacred project caught within and carrying forward the grander sacred vision of autonomous, self-directing, modern humanity.

This sacred project of American sociology took on a more muted hue during the mid-twentieth century, with the discipline's theoretical domination by the structural-functionalism of Talcott

---

18. Ward, 1893, *The Psychic Factor of Civilization*, Boston: Ginn, p. 114.
19. Hayes, 1915, *Introduction to the Study of Sociology*, New York: D. Appleton, p. 4.
20. Dealey, 1909, p. 503.

Parsons and his associates.[21] But the basic project had not fundamentally changed.[22] A mix of particular factors—such as the ascent of positivism in academia, America's postwar return-to-normalcy popular culture, the larger Cold War political context, and Parsons' own Protestant background and staid personality—simply gave sociology's spiritual mission a relatively more conservative, scientistic tone. Even so, new seeds of a more radical nature were germinating, particularly with various critical sociologies represented by the writings of C. Wright Mills and the neo-Marxist Frankfurt (Germany) School theorists, many of whom had come to New York to work at Columbia University.

A key turning point in this story was the disintegration of the theoretical supremacy of structural-functionalism in the 1960s, the fragmentation of American sociology into a multitude of different theoretical and methodological approaches, the influence of numerous profound cultural and social changes in the 1960s and 70s, and the massive growth of sociology in American higher education at the same time. The story is well known, so I will not retell it in detail.[23] Most important for my narrative is the fact that at roughly

21. George Steinmetz, 2007, "American Sociology Before and After World War II: The (Temporary) Settling of a Disciplinary Field," pp. 314–365 in Craig Calhoun, ed., *Sociology in America: A History*, Chicago: University of Chicago Press.

22. "The identity of 'sociologists' in the public mind was fixed during this era [the 1950s], and their message was this: differences between people, whether these were differences in suicide rates or rates of coronary occlusion, crime, poverty, and the like vary in relation to 'social facts' such as class position and race; therefore, 'society' is causally responsible for these differences. The moral of this story . . . was that the state ought to intervene" (Turner and Turner, 1990, p. 137).

23. Stephen Turner and Jonathan Turner, 1990, *The Impossible Science*, Newbury Park: Sage, pp. 133–178; Doug McAdam, 2007, "From Relevance to Irrelevance: the Curious Impact of the Sixties on Public Sociology," pp. 411–426, and Immanuel Wallerstein, 2007, "The Culture of Sociology in Disarray: The Impact of 1968 on U.S. Sociologists," pp. 427–437 in Craig Calhoun, ed., 2007, *Sociology in America: A History*, Chicago: University of Chicago Press; Alvin Gouldner, 1970, *The Coming Crisis of Western Sociology*, New York: Basic Books; George Ritzer, 1983, *Sociological Theory*, New York: Knopf, pp. 48–59.

the same time, (1) Parsonian sociology was attacked and discredited for, among many other problems, being too politically conservative; (2) American culture and society were undergoing major cultural and political turmoil and revolutions over black civil rights, the Vietnam war, rock-and-roll, student free speech, sexual values and morality, feminism, marriage and divorce, and other contentious issues, often propelled by Baby Boomer university students and some supportive faculty[24]; and (3) American higher education was expanding at an enormous pace to keep up with the demand set by Baby Boom demographics, which, along with many young people's interest in avoiding the military draft, was pushing massive numbers of youth through college and universities.

The first factor (Parson's demise) created an open space within American sociology—a kind of intellectual political opportunity[25]—for new, alternative, and sometimes radical approaches and voices to assert themselves. The second factor (turmoil and revolutions) caught up and radicalized many members of a whole generation of young Americans who led and followed (or perhaps simply sympathized with) these movements, protests, and upheavals and sought to continue to extend their influences further into mainstream American culture and society. The third factor (expanding higher education) provided an inviting opportunity for many such youth to turn their progressive interests and activism into stable careers, by going to graduate school, earning doctorates, and taking faculty positions in expanding colleges and universities where they could professionally learn about the social issues that concerned them and reproduce their own experiences by teaching younger college students the good news of purposive

24. See, for example, Bill Gamson's fascinating story on pp. 265–279 of Croteau, Hoynes, and Ryan, 2005.
25. Doug McAdam, 1999, *Political Process and the Development of Black Insurgency, 1930–1970* (2nd ed.), Chicago: University of Chicago Press.

social transformation—for whom, of all the academic disciplines most friendly to exactly that kind of attractive career in the 1970s, sociology was found to be foremost.[26]

In a relatively short time, sociology faculties were transformed. And the version of the sacred project of the discipline that emerged from that conversion was much closer to the one I have described above than that which Parsons or anyone before him oversaw. Infusing the older, received, optimistic heritage of Enlightenment, liberalism, and progressive social reformism with new energy and purpose were the (for white Northern liberals, exhilarating) experience of the black civil rights movement, a renewed theoretical interest in Marxism, and a moral commitment (begrudging among many "mere" liberals at first[27], but with increasing momentum and enthusiasm in due time) to feminist theory and politics. Peter Berger's social constructionism after the late 1960s provided a key theoretical legitimation for activism designed to transform social institutions (much of it against Berger's intentions). Sociology's sacred project was off and running again, with a renewed zeal brought by a new generation of young Baby Boomer teachers and scholars moving into higher education, which was dramatically expanding.

In due time, some of the more competent and ambitious from among this new generation of sociology faculty—along with their counterparts from other disciplines—moved up into positions of administrative authority within higher education.[28] These helped to reduce general institutional barriers in colleges and universities to the advance and entrenchment of spiritual projects such as

26. "Sociology became the academic program that absorbed many of the most politically committed students of the era" of the 1960s and 70s (Turner and Turner, 1990, p. 138).
27. I have heard horror stories from female sociologists who were graduate students in the 1970s about some of the most sexist male pig faculty mentors imaginable—enlightenment did not come fast or uniformly.
28. Jonathan Imber, 1995, "The Future of Sociology," *The American Sociologist*, Fall, p. 11.

I described above, despite a larger cultural and political retrenchment taking place in America in the latter 1970s and 1980s. Unlim-
ited abortion rights became adopted into sociology's sacred project.
By the 1980s and 1990s, American sociology started, haltingly at
first, to take on board (what has since been labeled) the GLBTQ
agenda; by the 2000s, GLBTQ advocacy had become *de rigueur* in
the discipline, a cause reservations about which only "homopho-
bic" moral Neanderthals might be conceived to hold. Neither poststructuralism nor postmodernism ever caught on in a big way in
mainstream American sociology—despite the promoting efforts of
some[29]—although, as I said above, their skeptically relativizing and
authority-hostile outlooks and sensibilities, which nicely comple-
ment the sacred project, have influenced the discipline in more diffuse, background ways.

In all of this, a kind of nostalgic status-hierarchy developed
among sociologists. Those who had personally participated in
the primal experiences of spiritual enlightenment—the civil
rights, student free speech, anti-Vietnam, and women's liberation
movements—became most revered. Those Boomers who lived
through that era and could attest to it were important too, even if
they had not personally been major participants. Younger sociologists had unfortunately "missed out" on the events of the 1960s'
"golden age," but many of them could still live that vicariously,
through studying, researching, and teaching about them. Opportunities to sort-of relive or recreate The Sixties, by engaging in (or
at least getting close enough to study) newly emerging progressive

29. For example, Steven Seidman, 1991, "The End of Sociological Theory: The Postmodern
Hope," *Sociological Theory*, 9: 138–146; Seidman, 1994, *Contested Knowledge: Social
Theory in the Postmodern Era*, Oxford: Blackwell; Steven Seidman and David Wagner,
1992, *Postmodernism and Social Theory*, Cambridge: Blackwell; Ben Agger, 1993,
Gender, Culture, and Power: Toward a Feminist Postmodern Critical Theory, New York:
Praeger; Agger, 2003, *Postponing the Postmodern: Sociological Practices, Selves, and The-
ories*, Lanham, MD: Rowman and Littlefield.

movements and protests, also provided younger sociologists a way to spiritually and morally connect to the former glorious era. This in part—along with much genuine moral and political conviction—helps to explain the appeal of many sociologists' interest in and various forms of involvement in and support of HIV/AIDS, Central America solidarity, anti-nuke, education reform, anti-globalization, GLBTQ, abortion rights, immigration rights, and other campaigns of activism. It also helps explain why Collective Behavior and Social Movements is one of the ASA's largest sections.

More pronounced in the latest version of American sociology's sacred project than in those animating previous eras is the moral centrality of the autonomous, self-directing, therapeutically oriented individual. The larger sacred vision remains to promote the good society. But a good society has come increasingly to be considered one that allows, nay, promotes and affirms the emancipation, equality, and moral affirmation of humans as autonomous, self-directing, individual agents seeking to live however they personally desire. That good society is one in which individuals are free to do as they please with regard to their identities, relationships, experiences, consumptions, and pleasures—again, without limit, as long as they don't obstruct anyone else doing the same. To keep things in perspective, however, this is merely a new emphasis, the seeds of which were planted long ago and have been growing along with the progressive unfolding of western modernity. Echoing themes above, Daniel Bell thus observes that modernity is essentially about "the rejection of a revealed order or natural order, and the substitution of the individual—the ego, the self—as the lodestar of consciousness." He writes:

> What we have here is the social reversal of the Copernican Revolution: if our planet is no longer the center of the physical universe and our earthly habitat is diminished in the horizons of

nature, the ego/self takes the throne as the center of the moral universe, making itself the arbiter of all decisions. There are no doubts about the moral authority of the self; that is simply taken as a given. The only question is what constitutes fulfillment of the self.[30]

According to contemporary sociology's sacred project, fulfillment of that self is realized by the autonomous self-determination of identity, relationships, experience, consumption, and pleasure. But those realizations all point to the individual self as the final moral authority and touchstone of reality. In this sense, the sacred project that dominates mainstream American sociology today is a natural, logical development of the inheritance of liberal, Enlightenment modernity—as it has passed through a host of particular, path-dependent contingencies. Getting here has just taken a long time, lots of technological developments, a number of horrific wars, economic prosperity, the spread of mass-consumer capitalism, and a bumptious generation of Baby Boomers.[31]

Is American sociology's sacred project inevitable? Does the innate logic of the sociological perspective in some way inherently lead to a commitment to this kind of disciplinary Durkheimian sacred cause? I think not. Some of European sociology's earliest thinking and instincts grew instead out of conservative and romanticist sensibilities.[32] Sociology as a disciplined way to understand, interpret, and explain the world can, I think, be framed by and put to many different spiritual, political, and cultural approaches and ends. Which among those approaches succeeds is significantly

30. Bell, 1990, "Resolving the Contradictions of Modernity and Modernism," *Society*, March/April, p. 43.
31. Here I subscribe somewhat to Ronald Inglehart's "post-materialist" thesis. Inglehart, 1989, *Cultural Shift in Advanced Industrial Societies*, Princeton: Princeton University Press.
32. Robert Nisbet, 1967, *The Sociological Tradition*, New York: Basic Books.

determined by the shared worldviews, interests, and purposes of those who institutionally populate, define, and reproduce the discipline.

In the American case, a particular history has shaped sociology. Baby Boomers with a bent toward its sacred project flooded the discipline in the 1960s and 70s, as I just explained. Since then, it has worked like this. American youth with an orientation to the spiritual project have been and still are more likely to go to college than not. Once in college, they find sociology to be the choice of majors that best resonates with their personal sensibilities and interests. Different students who are more interested in money choose to major in economics or business, those interested in law and formal political power major in political science, students interested in "how people work" major in psychology, but those interested in the sacred project I have described above (along with a mix of other types of students, not always the brightest) major in sociology. Among *that* pool of majors, the best, smartest, and most committed are then often attracted to graduate studies in sociology. Getting their own PhDs enables them to continue advancing sociology's spiritual project, to which they have become committed, through their own research, publishing, and the teaching of their own undergraduate students—all achieved within the context of a comfortable, stimulating, self-directed academic career. This, in short, is how the spiritual project of American sociology not only got started but is institutionally reproduced.

Chapter 5

Consequences

What are the consequences of American sociology's being and promoting a particular spiritual project? There are many, I think, some of which are good and some not so good. I wish here to focus on the latter, on what seem to me to be the more problematic consequences. Those sociologists who are true believers in the spiritual project may have trouble thinking of any problems with it, and many other sociologists will intuitively grasp and applaud the more positive possible results, so I need not discuss them here. Much less reflection has been given to the arguably problematic side of sociology's spiritual project, I think, so I focus on it in what follows. I will not make critiques based on mere personal differences in assumptions and beliefs, the kind of arguments that would only convince people who are already antagonistic to sociology's project. I will instead focus on certain troubling consequences that I believe impair sociology's being its best self in the academy and for the world beyond, which should concern people even if they otherwise are sympathetic to the sacred project. This is not about denunciations generated by fundamentally different presuppositions about reality. The concerns described below are instead those that most sociologists (and other academics) should understand and be concerned about, whatever they personally think of sociology's sacred project.

DISHONESTY

The first and most obvious problem is that—to the extent that sociology misrecognizes and somewhat masks the fact that it is and has a sacred project—the discipline is being dishonest with itself, its students, their parents, college and university administrators and donors, and American taxpayers. Sociology is caught in a conundrum here. It is and has a sacred project, but it cannot own up to that fact and say it in so many words. There is small chance that sociology will simply abandon its spiritual project, but it also cannot come completely clean with its various constituencies about it. So sociology is forced to finesse that difficult position by somewhat obscuring its commitment to its sacred project to itself and to others. Some of the more activist sociologists are comfortable publicly expressing the vision of their project—although would never admit to its being sacred, not to mention spiritual. But most normally prefer to think of sociology as merely the study of various aspects of society, whether or not it is "scientific," "interpretive," or something else. For them to come out and publicly admit that sociology is a sacred project would be unthinkable.

But if I am right here, the discipline is being duplicitous. It is engaging in doubletalk to hoodwink itself and others who would object to its being what it is. If I am right, sociology is living in denial about a crucial part of its basic identity and mission. What sociology is doing is essentially no different morally than religious proselytizers coming to one's door and pretending at first to be there for some other purpose than to convert you to their faith—and starting to preach only once they get inside the door. Only, things are actually worse with sociology, since its primary target for conversion to its sacred project about which it is not entirely upfront are 18- to 22-year-old college students, many of whom are captive audiences in classrooms and who are trying to figure out their own lives, identities, and commitments. Most of them and their parents are also paying money to—so they think—learn about the "science of society" when they take sociology classes. Only gradually and indirectly may it become apparent, however, that they are really being exposed to and socialized into a particular spiritual project that is fraught with hidden moral, philosophical, and political assumptions and ramifications. On purely ethical grounds and in the interest of protecting (whatever is left of) the institutional integrity of American higher education, it must be said that this situation is self-deceived, dishonest, and misleading of others who have placed trust in their colleges and universities and the departments and faculty they support and employ.

INTERNAL SELF-CONTRADICTIONS

I already mentioned above the idea of internal tensions present in sociology's sacred project. Let us think more about that idea. Sociology's sacred project implicates the discipline in some definite strains, what most ordinary people would call hypocrisies, revolving around the fact that the spiritual vision of the world and human life that it seeks to realize "out there" is rarely expressed within sociology itself. That is partly the result of the competitive, hierarchical, and bureaucratic character of American higher education. Even if sociologists wanted a revolution in the way they operate, that would be difficult if not impossible to accomplish. But sociology's tensions and hypocrisies are not all imposed from the outside: most sociologists seem happy to perpetuate them. What do I mean? I am talking about the incongruities between the strongly egalitarian impulses of sociology's sacred project and the highly unequal, stratified, status-oriented nature of sociology itself. For a discipline that is obsessed with social inequality as a moral wrong, American sociology turns out to be just as structured and driven by status hierarchy, rankings, elitism, excluding social processes, and protection of privilege as just about any other institution in society.

One of the primary concerns of most research-university departments of sociology, for instance, is their place in the departmental-status ranking system. Most decisions eventually come back as answers to this question: Will it help us maintain or improve our position in the competitive rankings? Even how departments distribute scarce resources to benefit status-enhancing scholarly research versus higher-quality undergraduate education is shaped by this determination to win (or at least not lose too badly) in the status ranking system Among sociologists and their departments on this point, egalitarianism and mutual affirmation are not to be found.[1]

Or consider the interpersonal social interactions among sociologists at the annual meetings of the American Sociological Association (ASA). They are tediously stratified.[2] "The best" sociologists largely circulate and talk with their own kind. Lower-status sociologists—measured mostly by the (lack of) prestige of their departments—may try to break into higher-status cliques but are

---

1. Yet to overtly state that some scholars and programs are simply better than others and should be consequently be differentially rewarded opens the door to admitting real and probably inevitable differences in quality, performance, and value of the work and output of different kinds of people, which sounds awfully like a functionalist or neo-liberal justification of natural or unavoidable socioeconomic inequality, and is freighted with major revisionary implications for sociology's spiritual project.
2. This language I owe to one of my brilliant graduate school mentors, Steve Rytina, now at McGill University.

usually unsuccessful. In fact, most of everyone's eye movements at the ASA meetings involve checking out other people's name tags, hung unceremoniously from lanyards around necks, to see if their names are recognizable and at what college or university they work. The extent to which people are greeted, merely smiled at, or ignored (with the pretense that nobody actually checked out anyone else's name tag) depends primarily on status-equality/inequality considerations. Heaven help the poor sociologist souls at the bottom.

I also bet that most "ordinary" sociologists are not aware that a circle of elite sociologists has organized its own exclusive, invitation-only professional association that meets somewhat surreptitiously alongside the ASA conferences.[3] I was never aware of it myself until I was by good fortune inducted into it. I am not a very good member of this club, but many of the people in it are good folks, and its dues are infinitely less expensive than those of ASA. The dinners, friendliness, and stimulating presentations we enjoy in it also provide a nice opportunity to be separated for a spell from the hoi polloi of our colleagues who attend the main conference.

Still, participants in the main ASA meeting have their own ways of maintaining status in-groups. Over a few decades of observation, I have noticed that different sections (at least those to which I have been involved) have their own cliques of insiders who manage to enjoy disproportionate shares of attention, esteem, and power. They occupy positions as section gatekeepers, recognizing or not recognizing newcomers, doling out or not doling out attention, defining who are the rising stars and who are not, and so on. My distinct impression, too, is that "membership" (or not) in these sections' inner circles is not irrelevant to the chances of being

3. Andrew Abbott has referred to it as "a secret handshake society of the movers and shakers in sociology" (Abbott, 2000, "Politics and Controversies in Sociology," Sociological Research Association dinner address, American Sociological Association, Washington, D.C., August 13.

fields (the average ASA member holds 2.96 section memberships[6]). And almost never do scholars from any one field or section pick an intellectual fight with those of another; that would be bad manners.

Furthermore, all of the old, tired battles, between quantitative versus qualitative, micro versus macro, structuralists versus interactionists, and so on, have been declared destructive and disarmed by peace-seeking "both/and" advocates enforcing informal ceasefires. Such truces are a good idea, I think, all in all, in view of the fact that the presuppositions mobilizing those battles were generally misconceived from the start. But the practical result has been the implementation in American sociology of a tacit peace treaty specifying that everyone should mostly think and do whatever he or she wishes in terms of methods, theory, and intent and not suggest that what anyone else is doing might be a problem (unless he or she violates the sacred project). "Everybody for themselves," in short—since there is room for anything and everything in the discipline, as long as some department is willing to hire the people doing it (again, as limited by the sacred project). One sociologist has named the current state of affairs our "Pax Wisconsana," after the large sociology department at Madison, Wisconsin, where a host of scholars work away on their different interests without much contention.[7]

A related reason why contemporary American sociology engages in so few meaningful, substantive intellectual debates is that sociology itself has become less theoretically interesting and philosophically reflective over time. Sociology today is simply not very strong on broader intellectual substance. Increasingly, sociology

---

6. Email from Justin Lini, ASA Program Coordinator, Governance and Information Systems (June 17, 2013). A total of 8,865 of ASA's 11,803 members (75.1 percent) have at least one section membership, with most having more than one, totaling to 26,216 section memberships.

7. John Levi Martin, 2011, *The Explanation of Social Action*, New York: Oxford University Press, p. 4.

graduate programs are turning out not intellectuals, but specialized technicians.[8] After a perfunctory sprint through some of the classics, most graduate students are drilled on methods and statistics, pushed through some seminar classes that review the major debates in certain fields, run up and down the MA-thesis staircase, given doctoral qualifying exams that summarize and criticize relevant literature in a few fields, and finally are pushed to write "doable" (read: narrow, unambitious, publishable) dissertations in order to prevent extended stays in their programs. Lately, dissertations often consist merely of three somewhat-related empirical papers intended to become journal articles, with an introduction and conclusion serving as bookends. Specific techniques are taught to graduate students in workshops about how to write an article that will "land" well (again, the Holy Grail being in *ASR* or *AJS*), which only a few are capable of doing. Time for sociology graduate students to read, think, and converse deeply is minimal, sometimes nonexistent. Professionalization and career development trump grad students' intellectual formation in what would be truly interesting and important questions. So, such a system does not produce many broadly read, thoughtful, intellectually interesting scholars and teachers. It produces technicians, as I said, who have learned more or less well how to play the faculty-career publishing game.

More broadly in sociology, philosophical questions that actually bear importantly on the purpose, value, and methods of sociology are ubiquitously considered irrelevant to "real" work in the discipline. Precious few sociologists of any generation now know enough philosophy to carry on even a short, informed discussion about matters of relevance and crucial importance to sociological work. "Just show me the data," "Why didn't you control for household

---

8. Thus contributing to what Albert O. Hirschman called our "specialization-induced intellectual poverty" (1977, *The Passions and the Interests*, Princeton: Princeton University Press).

income?," and "Screw patriarchy!" are instead the concerns of the day. As far back as the 1950s, "Grand Theory" was attacked, ridiculed, and ruled to be futile by influential sociologists C. Wright Mills and Robert K. Merton.[9] Promoting Mills' emancipatory "sociological imagination" and pursuing Merton's admonishment to develop "middle-range theory" have become the dominant, dual manifest interests in the discipline—neither of which, however, has developed in ways that make most of sociology very intellectually interesting. Sociology journals are filled with highly focused articles defending their correct techniques and making modest "contributions" to fairly minor in-house debates. The more technically expert ones submerge into inaccessibly sophisticated methods, usually not matched in quality of data or substantive significance of the theoretical questions addressed. In short, what is in fact most interesting about sociology lately—to reconnect to my larger thesis—is not really intellectual but, rather, spiritual. That, too, helps partly to explain the power of sociology's sacred project: it at least is interesting and invigorating.

In sum, most of American sociology has becoming disciplinarily isolated and parochial, sectarian, internally fragmented, boringly homogenous, reticently conflict-averse, philosophically ignorant, and intellectually torpid. Sociology lacks the kinds of sustained, fruitful, and intellectually meaningful clashes, struggles, and clarifications needed for a discipline such as itself to generate important scholarship and education. On matters about which sociologists do not agree, sometimes strongly disagreeing, the standard practice in force is "to each her own" and thus the avoidance of argument. Other matters about which most sociologists *do* agree help to make that suppression of lesser differences possible. And

9. Mills, 1959; Robert K. Merton, 1968, "On Sociological Theories of the Middle Range," *Social Theory and Social Structure*, New York: Free Press, pp. 39–72.

the most important of those agreements enabling sociology's social solidarity concerns its dominant sacred project. I know sociologists who snipe about others they see as holding only "naïvely liberal" or indefensibly "too-radical" version of the sacred project—just as still others also deride some colleagues, variously, as "bean counters" or "not very rigorous." But beneath those differences, most are committed to the discipline's sacred project itself, to one degree of intensity or another, and with some variance in emphasis. That is partly what makes sociologists care enough to snipe about their other relatively minor ideological and methodological differences.

In fact, returning to my main line of argument, I suggest that the hegemony of its sacred project in American sociology has the effect of deflecting and pushing out those invested in any other possible spiritual projects. In the end, the discipline is occupied by more than a critical mass of sociologists who on the surface have wildly divergent interests, methods, and pet theories, but who as a whole and slightly deeper take for granted the moral validity and superiority of their sacred project and pursue its practice and advance together. Some are passionately driven activists, embodying a progressive fundamentalism as purist as anyone on the religious right. Many others are true believers but more moderate in style, usually balancing placating and acquiescing to the demands of the passionate activists, but never acting in ways that call into question their own commitment to the project. Still others have their doubts but, given the sacred project's hegemonic power, and not wanting to put their reputations and careers at risk, engage in various forms of "voluntary" self-censorship to just go along. Those who don't are effectively ostracized. As a consequence, in the end, at its heart, when it comes to its most vital animating concerns, American sociology turns out to be a quite homogenous place with little room for intellectual, moral, and sacred diversity, challenge, argument, and mutual learning across real differences. Sociology has at

This might not be a problem if sociology operated with many different projects and worldviews that generated different perspectives on reality. Each could in such a context of real pluralism make its genuine contribution, all could hash out their differences together, and our understanding of the social world would be that much more complete. Unfortunately, since American sociology has one dominant sacred project, and since those who do not subscribe to it are more or less marginalized, in the end the discipline operates with only one set of analytic glasses fitted with one very particular prescription for its lenses, which allows those who wear it to focus only on one part of the possible full range of vision. Some of the real social world is brought into focus; some of it is not.[14]

More troublingly, the particular perspective, interests, and focus that sociology's spiritual project determines are actually sometimes *misleading* in the understandings of the social world they suggest. The problem is not always simply a matter of this project affording us some limited knowledge and other projects providing other knowledge, all of which is complementary. Some perspectives actually *misguide* us into making false assumptions, thinking in the wrong categories, asking the wrong questions, and looking at the wrong evidence. When they do so, they foster *mis*understandings and inadequate explanations. American sociology's sacred project does this to our sociological analyses sometimes. It compels us to set up our problems incorrectly, to miss important factors at work, to force explanations that fit the given assumptions of the project

14. "The insularity of its political orthodoxies has left sociology as an undergraduate (and I expect graduate) subject in ignorance of both scientific findings in other fields as well as political developments in the United States and throughout the world, except as such fields and (other than left-wing) political convictions can be dismissed and attacked as sexist, racist, and retrograde, effectively stifling serious debate and serious acknowledgement of social change" (Jonathan Imber, 1999, "Values, Politics, and Science: The Influence of Social Movements on Sociology—Other-Directed Rebels," *Contemporary Sociology*, May, pp. 255–260).

CONSEQUENCES

rather than to be open to think imaginatively in other, potentially more fruitful, ways. In the end, when this happens, it produces substandard sociology.

What are specific examples of this process at work? For one illustration, the sacred project of American sociology directs those who belong to it and who carry it forward to conceive of social reality ontologically as consisting of "individuals" and "society." In this model, the interests and desires of individuals and society are assumed to be in conflict, and so the relationship between the two is considered to be individuals *versus* society. This is what is known as the "homo-duplex" model of social reality, which was adopted by most of sociology's founders.[15] Important to realize about this model is that it is not necessarily Obvious Truth, but a very *particular* conception of things inherited from a *specific* historical tradition, which is *presupposed* by those who believe it, not simply naïvely generated and validated by empirical facts, but instead *brought to* the empirical world as part of a larger a priori package of ideas and used to make sense of it. The specific package of ideas from which the homo-duplex model derives is western liberal individualism. There are, it should go without saying, alternative human and social ontologies. Given its theoretical assumptions, the crucial basic problems and questions are framed as something like, "What limits must be placed on the demands of society to protect individual liberty?" and "How can individuals protect their freedom in the face of social institutions—especially states—that threaten to absorb and oppress them (at least until they are taken over by us good guys)?" The fundamental reality is presupposed in this theory to be one of legitimate individual autonomy versus threatening sociopolitical demands and coercion. The basic problem then is how to integrate individuals into a workable social order

15. Smith, 2015; Jonathan Fish, 2013.

without violating their rightful freedoms. This presupposed social ontology of individuals-versus-society has structured the basic sociological vision from the start and still does today. Its categories, interests, and expectations control how basic social reality is seen and ordered, what count as important puzzles to solve, what kind of evidence will be persuasive, what an adequate theory will look like, and when a satisfactory explanation has been found. Viewing the world through this particular paradigm brings into focus certain important dimensions of social reality but also obscures others. If sociology were less beholden to its particular sacred project, and to the social ontologies that it presupposes (in this case, the homo-duplex model of individuals versus society), I believe it would be able to think more creatively, insightfully, and fruitfully about the complexities of real human societies.[16] Insofar as the dominance of sociology's spiritual project prevents that, sociology's vision and thinking are myopically narrowed and some of the puzzles it takes on are misconstrued.

Another example: An important aspect of American sociology's sacred project, as I mentioned above, is the desire to displace the authority of traditional, institutional religion (*especially* Christianity, being the most irrational and oppressive of them all) with the authority of secular, rational, empirical (social) science and secular movements for social and political justice. For this reason, it was incredibly easy for the *hypothesis* of secularization theory to morph in the minds of sociologists into an absolute confidence in secularization as an inexorable historical inevitability, which teetered among many sociologists on (and sometimes over) the brink of normatively recommending and celebrating secularization.[17]

16. Smith, 2015.
17. Jeffrey Hadden, 1987, "Toward Desacralizing Secularization Theory," *Social Forces*, 65(3): 587–611; Peter Glasnerr, 1977, *The Sociology of Secularisation*, London: Routledge and Kegan Paul, pp. 2, 64.

For most of the twentieth century, therefore, American sociology largely ignored religion and its role and impact on human social, political, and economic life. Sociology graduate students in the mid-twentieth century who wanted to study religion were routinely told by their advisors, "Why study something that is dying? It's like studying dinosaurs. It doesn't matter."[18] With such a sacred-project-driven confidence in secularization both as empirical fact and normative good, sociologists spent much of a century disregarding religion empirically and theoretically.

Then a funny thing happened in the late 1970s: religion "returned" to public life with a resurgent vengeance and has remained there ever since (of course, religion had actually never really gone away). So, just when sociology was most needed to make good sense of a born-again president, the Iranian revolution, liberation theology, a world-transforming Catholic pope, the religious right, Poland's Catholic Solidarność movement, militant "base communities" in Latin America, the cultural resurgence of American evangelicalism, revolutionary priests in Nicaragua and El Salvador, the spread like wildfire of Pentecostalism in the Global South, the successful theological challenge to South African apartheid, the church's undermining of Eastern European communism, the growth of militant Islamism, the explosion of religion in China, and so many other world-historical events and processes, guess how well equipped American sociology was to help understand and explain them? Abysmally. Few in American sociology possessed any of the right conceptual, theoretical, and analytic tools needed to understand well what was going on in the world. For the longest time, many sociologists simply ignored these events, or insisted that all of this represented merely the final death throes of

---

18. Versions of this story have been recounted to me multiple times by scholars of a certain generation, including Wade Clark Roof and Edward Cleary, among others.

religion before the final triumph of secularization; or they simply morally condemned and publicly denounced with resentment the rise of Jerry Falwell, Ralph Reed, and Pat Robertson. In short, in the 1980s, especially, American sociology got caught with its scholarly pants down (or skirts up), and it has taken decades to try to get them pulled up (or down) enough again to perhaps make a useful contribution to properly understanding religion around the globe.[19] It remains uncertain whether American sociology will be capable of ever doing that, despite some admirable tries.

Why did sociology fail so pathetically at the crucial moment, when and where it should have shone brightly at its best, when it came to religion? Because for most of the century previously it had simply not cared about religion, accepted a simplistic theoretical dismissal of religion, and so ignored religion as a social fact. In retrospect, as a matter of scientific, scholarly responsibility, that failure was inexcusable and embarrassing—at least it *ought* to have been. Precious few American sociologists have owned up to it, however, and offered any attempt at an explanation. And that is because the real explanation is even more embarrassing than the fact of the failure: a particular secular sacred project to which American sociology is devoted blinded (and continues to blind) the discipline to the ongoing reality and importance of religion as a social fact of political, economic, and cultural consequence. This is another example of sociology's sacred project not simply tilting its faculty to the political left but actually blinding its social scientific vision, distorting its cognitive capacities for understanding and explanation, and so causing failures in its basic disciplinary mission.

19. See Christian Smith, Brandon Vaidyanathan, Nancy Tatom Ammerman, José Casanova, Hilary Davidson, Elaine Howard Ecklund, John Evans, Philip Gorski, Mary Ellen Konieczny, Jason Springs, Jenny Trinitapoli, and Meredith Whitnah, 2013, "Twenty-Three Theses on the Status of Religion in American Sociology," *Journal for the American Academy of Religion*," December, pp. 1–36.

A third example: The sacred project of American sociology is so heavily dependent upon a strong "social-construction-of-reality" perspective that it is prevented by its own spiritual commitments from seeing and understanding certain aspects of human life that constructionism misses, but that a more realist approach more naturally sees and grasps. Sociology's sacred endeavor is wedded to social constructionism in particular because that theory "de-naturalizes" the social world in a way that makes it susceptible to purposeful human transformation through social movements, political programs, reforms, and revolutions. That outlook perfectly fits the viewpoint and interests of the dominant sacred project. Social constructionism tells us a lot that is true. But sociologists—carried away "by the spirit," as it were—often take it too far. Nearly all of reality is talked about as if it were socially constructed, which is ludicrous.[20] Social constructionism must be properly set into context by a more basic and adequate framework of realism—critical realism, to be specific. But realism is threatening to the sacred project dominating sociology. That is because realism recognizes certain natural orders, structures, tendencies, human conditions, causal mechanisms, social processes, possibly moral facts, and so on that regulate and direct the nature and dynamics of human personal and social life, as well as the natural order. And that suggests to many sociologists what are to them the intolerably polluted ideas of "essences," "nature," "given orders," and other heretical concepts that oppressively threaten to place real limits on individual human autonomy, unconstrained self-creation, and sovereign self-direction. This helps explain why many American sociologists are deeply suspicious of critical realism, despite the fact that, when actually understood, it stands out

---

20. Smith, 2010, *What is a Person?: Rethinking Human Personhood, Social Life, and the Moral Good from the Person Up*, Chicago: University of Chicago Press, esp. pp. 119–219.

far and away as the best meta-theoretical framework for social science among all of its rivals.

So, innumerable American sociologists find themselves drawn to strong versions of social constructionism not because they make the most sense but because of their good fit with the dominant sacred vision. But that constructionism, when not framed and limited by the right kind of realism, not only places blinkers on the sociological perspective but positively misleads sociologists' perceptions, understandings, and explanations of social reality. And in this way—as I have explained more fully elsewhere[21]—sociology's spiritual vision actually distorts the discipline's capacity to do its proper job as well as it might and ought. In short, sociology's spiritual vision often proves to be not merely a disciplinary hallmark but a scholarly liability.

Finally, a fourth example: American sociology reflects an unsettled, equivocal view of the state as a social institution that prevents it, in my view at least, from seeing and thinking clearly enough about the goods and limits of government. On the one hand, sociology's spiritual vision views "the state" as frequently controlled by the rich and powerful and therefore unable to establish equality and justice in society. Frequently the state is seen and portrayed as callous, inept, and corrupted by elite interests. The state is conceptualized as the agent of socially legitimate violence and so essentially a malign force in human life. On the other hand and simultaneously, American sociology's spiritual vision looks to the state to finally solve most of the social, economic, cultural, and political problems it is committed to ending. Great confidence most sociologists place in government programs, policies, and regulations (and courts to enforce them when administrations grow weak-kneed) to end discrimination, fairly redistribute wealth, establish universal equality,

21. Smith, 2010, 2014.

achieve comprehensive justice, and legislate away exploitation and oppression. So, oddly, the state simultaneously wears a white hat and a black hat. And the only way as far as I can see that this contradiction is (seemingly) resolved is by embracing the perennial leftist (and far right-wing) confidence that once the currently corrupt state is stormed and transformed, once government power has been taken over by those on the side of truth and righteousness (us), then the black hat will be cast away forever and the state will don the white hat only, as it establishes justice, equality, and the acceptance of all by all, riding off heroically into the sunset. (Never mind the practical results that such naïve confidence has often if not normally produced, illustrated by the likes of Maximilien de Robespierre, Adolf Hitler, Joseph Stalin, and Mao Zedong.) Meanwhile, this unstable compound of deep suspicion and naïvely optimistic confidence needed to make sense of the state has the result, I observe, of clouding sociologists' visions in black-and-white ways that harm how they understand and explain the many social problems that disturb and activate them. In short, reasonable thought and analysis are sometimes confused by sacred experience and expectation, at least in the case and of the sort that animates American sociology.

CORRUPTION OF THE PEER-REVIEW PROCESS

Sociology as a social science depends for its legitimacy upon the integrity of the impartial, (usually double-)blind peer-review system to ensure scholars' and the public's trust that its published scholarship represents the highest-quality science drawn from the broadest swath of best studies possible. That system depends upon all participants acting fairly to prioritize the scientific quest for truth, as most clearly as it can be known, over their own personal interests, pet beliefs, and political commitments. Transcending the diverse, particular opinions, ideologies, and allegiances personally held by the multitude of social scientists must stand, for this system to function well, a shared higher commitment to the best possible methods, evidence, and reasoning—whatever findings they produce. Everyone involved has to let research findings stand (until improved upon) that are produced by the best available, commonly shared scholarly standards to which all are committed. Everyone needs to remain open to the possibility that what he or she previously believed might be demonstrated wrong by good new evidence. Without these dynamics in play, sociology—and every other (social) science—quickly degenerates into tribalism, posturing, and domination though coercive power.

I believe we have reason to think that certain aspects, at least, of American sociology's sacred project, especially its more sectarian expressions, place at risk the integrity of this peer-review process. If so, then it is a grave matter. To be clear, there is in my view nothing about people pursuing a sacred project per se that prevents them from honoring and supporting scientific peer-review systems. In principle, many sacred projects are entirely compatible with shared reason, the authority of good evidence and arguments, and a commitment to finding the truth, whatever it may happen to be. Some sacred projects in fact place at their centers the search for truth—whatever the truth may be—and the epistemological humility needed to keep us open to improving our human understandings of the truth. But not all do. Some sacred projects are so doggedly committed to advancing their particular, packaged views of believed orthodoxies that they can become blinded to good evidence that problematizes their truth-packages and intolerant of other people whom they believe impede their sacred missions. American sociology's sacred project has those tendencies and, increasingly, it seems to me, more sociologists are acting upon them. How so?

Let us return first to the Regnerus affair described above to consider one important example. Most obvious in that episode was the attack on Regnerus himself. Less obvious but no less important was the assault on the integrity of the double-blind peer-review process involved in those attacks. Recall that Regnerus' paper had been evaluated by six blind reviewers, all of whom recommended publication. Recall that the quality of Regnerus' sample was, though not perfect, superior to any other that had been used to answer this research question prior to his study. Nothing in the review process was unusual or dubious, a fact that even the appointed auditor of it, who was extremely hostile to Regnerus and his work, later had to admit. In short, there was no good reason to subject the review of this paper to any extraordinary scrutiny. Respectable members of the journal's editorial board should have conferred with the editor to confirm the facts and then stood up to publicly defend the review process, together telling what was by then becoming an academic lynch mob to back off and respect the established process.

But that is not what happened. Instead, the political pressures overwhelmed the established system and authorities. The journal's editor finally agreed to appoint one member of his publication board to conduct a thorough investigation and produce a report. Unfortunately, in order to appease the critics, one of the most (as I will show below) resentful, slanderous, and activist sociologists available was appointed to this task. When I directly questioned this choice, I was told that an acknowledged firebrand activist was intentionally selected for this task, instead of a more balanced, fair-minded scholar, in order to maximize the investigation's "credibility" among the crowd that was raising hell. The already compromised process was deliberately pandering to the angry mob, in short. The authorized investigation was conducted and, as I said above, the review process was exonerated—nothing, it was admitted, was notably wrong with the process by which the article had been reviewed and accepted for publication. The *Chronicle of Higher Education* thus reported the following about the audit:

> [The auditor] did not find that the journal's normal proce-
> dures had been disregarded, or that the Regnerus paper had
> been inappropriately expedited to publication, as some critics
> have charged. He also vigorously defended . . . the editor. "If
> I were in [the editor's] shoes," he writes, "I may well have made
> the same decisions." Because the reviewers were unanimously
> positive, [the editor] had little choice but to go ahead with pub-
> lication, according to [the auditor]. He goes on: "My review of
> the editorial processing of the Regnerus . . . paper . . . revealed
> that there were no gross violations of editorial procedures—
> the papers were peer-reviewed, and the 'peers' for papers on
> this topic were similar to what you would expect at *Social Sci-
> ence Research*."

That was the official report.[22] The personal response of the appointed investigator, however, reframed the audit's results in the
same breath by immediately and publicly adding that "it's bullshit"
and that "scholars who should have known better failed to recuse
themselves from the review process."[23] The auditor had of course
never been commissioned or authorized to use the report as a public
platform to proclaim and lend gravity to his own personal feelings
about the article. But that did not prevent him from exploiting that
opportunity in the limelight to shift the focus from the integrity
of the review process to his own personal evaluation of the article

22. See Darren Sherkat, 2012, "The Editorial Process and Politicized Scholarship: Monday
Morning Editorial Quarterbacking and a Call for Scientific Vigilance," *Social Science
Research*, 41:1346–1349.
23. Tom Bartlett, "Controversial Gay-Parenting Study is Severely Flawed, Journal's Audit
Finds," *Chronicle of Higher Education*, July 26, 2012.

itself, even though the latter somewhat contradicted what the official report showed. Since the official audit did not vindicate the cause the auditor championed, it was apparently necessary to resort to personal comments undermining the paper to keep the inquisition alive. In fact, the appointed auditor on July 15, 2012, actually personally emailed one of the activist "journalists" who was also pushing hard for investigations of Regnerus on various fronts, writing:

> Regnerus produced some exceptionally distorted and inferior research that should not have been published in a major general interest journal (yes, you can quote me on that)—but that is not a violation of anything. He just sucks and is a political whore. He'll pay for it later in reputation loss. . . . Believe me, I know there is a vast right wing conspiracy and that Mark Regnerus is a part of it! . . . I am almost finished with my audit response, and I will send it to you very soon. . . . I want to thank you and everyone in the activist community for keeping this on the front burner. This will make a difference. Until this Regnerus controversy, people thought I was a fucking psycho! Well, now they know! How did this study get through peer review? The peers are right wing Christianists! I've been telling people this for a fucking decade! And, this was all about that.[24]

In the end, the official report that validated the integrity of the review process was essentially ignored in the activist press, in some of the general academic press, and on various sociological blogs,

24. Wood, 2013, pp. 177–178; originally posted online by Scott Rose, "BOMBSHELL: Editor Darren Sherkat Admits Peer Review Failure of Invalid, Anti-Gay Regnerus Study," The New Civil Rights Movement (blog), July 27, 2012, http://thenewcivilrightsmovement. com/bombshell-editor-darren-sherkat-admits-peer-review-failure-of-invalid-anti-gay-regnerus-study/politics/2012/07/27/43778—although the original posting containing all quotes and cites may no longer be available online.

and the auditor's personal evaluative comments ("It's bullshit") were interpreted in their worst light and emblazoned in headlines like, "Regnerus Is 'Disgraced,' Anti-Gay Parenting Study 'Deeply Flawed' Says Chief Reviewer," "Mark Regnerus Revealing His True Colors As Anti-Gay Activist," "Regnerus Sham Study Part of Shady Evangelical Effort To Infiltrate Academia," "Rigorous about Regnerus: a Case Study in Bullshit Detection," and "Mark Regnerus was Coached to Pretend his Study wasn't Biased."[25] Many of the Internet articles covering the audit contained glaring inaccuracies and gross exaggerations. In this smear campaign, the truth proved a greater casualty than it usually suffers in war. The entire affair was driven by a determination to destroy a credible scholar whose research was (needlessly) interpreted as threatening to a sacred vision—no matter how much distortion and character assassination it would take—and with the active cooperation of many academic sociologists.[26]

25. David Badash, May 29, 2013, http://thenewcivilrightsmovement.com/regnerus-is-disgraced-anti-gay-parenting-study-deeply-flawed-says-appointed-reviewer/politics/2013/05/29/67639; Evan Hurst, April 11, 2013, http://www.truthwinsout.org/news/2013/04/34370/; Jeremy Hooper, May 18, 2013, http://www.glaad.org/blog/rigorous-about-regnerus-case-study-bullshit-detection; Hannah Moch, April 12, 2013, http://www.glaad.org/blog/mark-regnerus-was-coached-pretend-his-study-wasnt-biased.

26. Doug Massey rightly noted, in reflection on the event: "Science never rests on a single study. It realizes that any single piece of research might be flawed or misleading in a variety of ways. The best we can do is subject a piece to peer review and hope for the best, recognizing that peer review is itself an imperfect process. In the longer term, however, science works well because the truth eventually comes out when people generate contradictory findings or fail to replicate, or discover methodological flaws in the original findings. Such would probably have been the case for the Regnerus article in the usual course of events. Papers based on questionable data and methods get published all the time, but in most cases they are forgotten, ignored, or disregarded if they fail to stand up to scrutiny. In this case, critics of the Regnerus paper took their critique to the Internet and it went viral, probably doing more to publicize the views articulated in the paper than would have ever occurred if the usual academic conventions were followed. In my view, this episode yields several conclusions," the first of which Massey observes, is that, "science has become extremely politicized" (Massey, 2012, "Comment," *Social Science Research*, 41: 1378).

But researchers and authors are not the only ones now at risk. Activists in the Regnerus debacle not only also went after the editor of the journal, *Social Science Research*, but also his email communications with the reviewers of the Regnerus paper, in order to be able to "expose" them too.

For present purposes, the crucial point to learn from that sorry episode is this: *It has now become acceptable to launch an investigation of the journal review process by which any sociology article is published as long as enough readers do not like the findings of the article and can mobilize enough protesters to pressure an editor into submission.* With this, we have turned a decisive corner toward the tolerability of *scholarly review by mob intimidation.* And that is the end of credible social science. The consequences of this episode are colossal and malign. So why are more sociologists not disturbed by what happened? It seems that either their personal sympathies for the attack on Regnerus were strong enough to enable them to ignore the destructive meaning of this event, or most were simply too intimidated by the political forces mobilized against Regnerus to say or do anything publicly in resistance.[27] Either way, the stink is putrid.

Editors have now been put on notice that their editorial judgments have no decisive authority and that their own editorial board may not back them up even when their practices have been squeaky clean. Prospective reviewers now know that their professional evaluations of the merits of scholarly papers they are asked to review are now in principle in doubt and are, in fact, subject to external questioning, reconsideration, and possible exposure by individuals

27. Among the many things that need to happen to help fix sociology, in my view, is that the more seriously "scientific" minority of sociologists—many of whom have a great deal of power in the discipline—need to get more backbone and start individually and collectively standing up to their "true believer" colleagues and to non-academic activists intruding into sociology, in order to pull the discipline back in more sane directions.

appointed to audit them who have been selected to pander to activist antagonists. Furthermore, consumers of articles in sociology journals now have good cause to suspect that the social science research published in them may be biased by the fears, intimidations, and career-security concerns that the Regnerus uproar has raised. The acids spilled by this incident, and others American sociology's spiritual mission might provoke, have astonishing powers to corrode the integrity of sociology's scholarly peer-review process, and therefore reasons to trust it. We would be foolish to write the Regnerus incident off as an isolated anomaly: it is indicative of a real, larger problem.

Stories told informally about the peer-review system working in suspicious ways—perhaps even in ideologically biased ways—are not uncommon to hear. Some of that may be sour grapes among rejected authors, but I doubt all of it is. Yet documenting cases of corrosion of the peer-review system is not easy, since all of the parties involved have strong incentives not to bring them to light. Paper reviewers are not going to admit that their personal politics and ideologies affected their judgments. Journal editors gain nothing by exposing problems in their review systems. And authors whose papers are discriminated against illegitimately have many reasons not to make an issue over it. They know they will be submitting more papers in the future, wish to stay on good terms with editors, do not want to be seen as troublemakers, and generally face every pressure that prevents most potential whistleblowers anywhere from becoming actual whistleblowers. I do not mean to suggest that sociology's journal peer-review system is rampant with corruption, but I do think it is vulnerable to pernicious influences exerted by some scholars who are driven by some of the less admirable aspects of sociology's sacred project. The Regnerus debacle shows that it can happen and has happened. The potential for more abuse is real.

Consider the Pandora's box that these kinds of incidents and questions open. I know of one paper about the relationship between involvement in the Boy Scouts of America and subsequent well-being in life, the analysis of which showed a positive relationship between scouting and well-being. It was recently rejected by a journal on the basis of four reviews. The reviews praised the article but also raised a number of valid criticisms; my own sense is that the paper's rejection was warranted for legitimate methodological reasons. Curiously, however, two of the four reviewers went out of their way, while discussing possible problems of sample selection, to point out (one of them did so twice in two separate paragraphs) that the Scouts discriminate against homosexuals and non-religious members, that this policy of discrimination has raised a lot of social and political controversy, and that participation in the Scouts has become dominated by religious "fundamentalists."[28] On the face of it, these observations were not unrelated in principle to a valid observation and question about the sample—not that the differences involved would in my view have any significant effects on the study's findings. However, this methodological question could have been raised by the reviewers just as clearly without drawing nearly as much attention to the gay-rights controversy surrounding the Boy Scouts as they did. The particular highlighting of these discriminating features of the Boy Scouts as an organization in these scholarly reviews stood out to the paper's authors and stands out to me, given the present political climate and the sensitivity to such issues within sociology, in view of the article's findings about positive associations between Scouting and well-being. In a former

28. Since one of the major supporters of the Boy Scouts is the mainline Protestant denomination, the United Methodist Church, that association with "fundamentalists" is factually inaccurate; it also reflects a journalistic-like ignorance of American religion to call Mormons, another major supporter of the Scouts, "fundamentalists," even if they are socially conservative in many ways—yet another example of many sociologists' broad ignorance of religion.

era, I would have believed that these highlighted references had nothing whatsoever to do politically with the reviewers' or editor's evaluation of the paper. Lately, however, we have reason for second thoughts about that.

One published account tells of how a paper with a solid research finding that showed a positive association between higher involvement with religious activities and lower crime rates was ultimately rejected by a journal editor, after a solid revise-and-resubmit decision and an extremely careful revision that responded well to all of the reviewers' concerns, and despite two very positive original and final reviews. Surprised, the paper's author called the editor to find out what happened. The editor admitted frankly that the paper was rejected solely on the grounds that a third reviewer, described by the editor as "a heavyweight" in the field, had said just that, "There is something wrong with this paper, I don't know what it is, I can't put my finger on it, but something is not right." Now, scholarly heavyweights rarely have trouble finding problems in papers—that is, unless the problems have to do with issues that cannot be publicly admitted, such as one's personal prejudices against religion and inability to believe that religion might produce positive social goods, such as lower crime rates. This third review, the author said, was the kind that his graduate-school mentor had in warning called an "FLR": "a funny-looking review . . . that makes little sense and not only reflects the bias of the reviewer, but how uncomfortable they are with the findings."[29] Some scholarly papers contain findings that challenge the orthodoxies of sociology's sacred project. In this

---

29. Byron Johnson, 2011, *More God, Less Crime: Why Religion Matters and How it Could Matter More*, Conshohocken, PA: Templeton, pp. 171–175. Similar stories about seemingly groundless negative reviews and editors' strange rejection decisions for papers demonstrating empirically that "religion matters" continually accumulate and are informally shared among sociology-of-religion scholars—some, but in my view, certainly not all of which, can be explained by sour grapes over having one's paper rejected, which no author likes.

case, it was the finding that religion is not an unmitigated bad that would best be swept away by the forces of rational, universal, enlightened secularism. And, no matter how potentially methodologically solid such findings are, many sociologists caught up in their sacred project have difficulty evaluating them fairly. What they are certain that they personally *know* about religion trumps what the empirical data say, and some way is found to turn in to the editor a negative review.[30] When that happens, the impartial, double-blind, peer-review process—which is sociology's only lifeline to genuine scientific legitimacy—is corrupted.[31]

30. The blindness of some sociologists to the genuine importance of religion in many parts of human social, political, and economic life—seemingly for no other reason than that religion is not important, or even is a target of dislike, in their own personal lives—can be astounding. I recently reviewed a very good sociology book, for example, that argued strongly that sociology needs to re-orient itself to what matters to ordinary people. Oddly, however, the book nearly completely ignored religion as something that (in fact) matters to very many people, mentioning it only in a few disparaging remarks. The author's selective capacity to disregard religion in way that violated his own clear argument was remarkable (Christian Smith, 2013, review of Andrew Sayer, "Why Things Matter to People: Social Science, Values, and Ethical Life," *Journal of Critical Realism*, 12(2): 255–259); also see Christian Smith, 2011, "Beyond Ignorance and Dogma: On Taking Religion Seriously," *Footnotes*, March, p. 14; Ryan Cragun, 2012, "In Favor of Relevance: When Religious Studies Matter," *Footnotes*, April, p. 10; Christian Smith, 2012, "Response to 'In Favor of Relevance,'" *Footnotes*, July/August, p. 14.
31. To be sure, science itself is not a neutral, objective activity, but a human practice profoundly determined by specific moral commitments and worldviews. We do good science never by taking up residence in some alleged neutral space, but by together committing ourselves to highly particular moral ideals—to truth, honesty, accountability, openness to persuasion, civility of argument, and so on (Michael Polanyi, 1974, *Personal Knowledge*, Chicago: University of Chicago Press; Polanyi, 2009, *The Tacit Dimension*, Chicago: University of Chicago Press). This presupposes virtues learned and taught in a very particular kind of morally shaped discursive community. Recognizing the particularities of all knowledge-perspectives, however, should not drive us into epistemic relativism, but rather a shared recognition of the need for a common commitment to and cultivation of scientific virtues and moral practices. The particularities of different perspectives and visions will come out in different people's work, which is inevitable and legitimate—as long as everyone is not trying to hide that or allow it to distort their scholarship. Even then, a shared commitment to the common good of humanity needs to animate all of our scholarly work. Science can operate on behalf of the human good, but must not be hijacked and manipulated to immediately promote

Another different kind of concern on the same general topic: the Internet has created whole new means by which the traditional double-blind peer-review system may be and already is in some ways, I believe, being undermined. I am referring here to the spate of new sociology blogs that have sprung up in recent years in which handfuls of sociologists publicly comment upon and often criticize published works in the discipline. The commentary published on these blogs operates outside of the gatekeeping systems of traditional peer review. All it takes to make that happen is for one or more scholars who want to amplify their opinions into the blogospheres to set up their own blogs and start writing. There are no editors, editorial boards, peer reviewers, accountability to associations, or shared standards of ethics (in fact, the ASA's published Code of Ethics as of this writing is entirely inadequate for the Internet age). This situation essentially "empowers" any sociologist to criticize, even smear, any other sociologist's work as he or she pleases, with little accountability to anyone for it. If this were conducted properly, it could provide a benefit to the discipline. But, in my observation, the discipline's sacred project sometimes steers how these sociology blogs operate in highly problematic directions.

The most accurate way to state what can and sometimes does happen is to say that these blogs are used to conduct *extra-institutional vigilante peer reviews*. No journal or book review editor has asked any of these sociologists to review a paper or book. Which publications get critiqued and sometimes lambasted is entirely up to the blog owners and authors. This makes them highly susceptible to conducting not reviews of a breadth of literatures

sectarian views and ideologies. Such a position thus both defends a very high view of science (unlike many perspectivalists) while recognizing the inescapably subjective, particular, partial, biased position of all human knowers (unlike many proponents of scientism), a tension that is held in dynamic fruitfulness by a smart commitment to (critical) realism and the epistemological humility that comes with that commitment.

but selective attacks on publications that the blog writers happen to want to discredit. Obviously—in part because Internet blogs are many steps removed from official professional means of communication (hence, the *extra-institutional*)—their writers' personal agendas, politics, and even intense animosities can and do shape who gets selected for criticism and how fair the critiques and sometimes condemnations and denigrations of them are. This is where the *vigilante* part comes in. If another sociologist whose person or research findings one hates manages through the established peer-review system to get something published, one can assail him or her post hoc on the Internet with varying degrees of reasonable evidence and contempt, and validate the established ideological views of blog readers who like what one has to say—all without the least professional accountability. I have seen this happen in different cases on at least four different such websites. Some are (or at least appear to be) more professional and evidence-based—although in the end these can conduct and have in fact conducted perfectly snarky and sometimes vicious smears of colleagues. Others engage in attacks that seem more fictional in their outlandishness than real. Here is one such actual blog post, presented verbatim, in full, and for present purposes (though not otherwise) worth reading closely. This Internet blog post, note, was written and published by *the very same sociologist who was officially appointed to conduct the audit of the peer-review process of Mark Regnerus' controversial article* (10 months later), about which I wrote above:

"Let's All Laugh At The Christianist "Sociologists" With An Actual Sociologist [Me] Who Is Not Dumb!"

May 31, 2013—*A guest post from your comrade [. . .], a real live sociologist who accidentally thoroughly discredited the bullshit Regnerus "homos kill their babies" study.* Hey Wonketteers, remember in "college" when you took that course in "sociology"?

You know, the one taught by an androgynous hippy, and where you learned about inequality and racism and sexism, and how to become a communist homosexican? Obviously, you passed or you wouldn't be reading Wonkette! Well, would you believe that there is an Association of Christians Teaching Sociology? No fucking way, you say? Way! Indeed, their keynote speaker for this weekend's meeting is Marky Mark Regnerus — author of the Bullshit Gay Parenting study! No doubt Marky Mark will be telling his fans about his bullshit study, where he got nearly a million dollars from his boyfriend Bradley Wilcox's foundation to prove that gays and lesbians make their children homos by molesting them and cause all manner of negative outcomes, too. He did this bullshit study by trolling through an online, non-random marketing study where he asked the trolls who munch Cheetos and fill out questionnaires for monies if their mom or dad ever had a "romantic relationship" with someone of the same sex? Out of 13k non-random trolls, about 245 (depending on which codebook you believe) said yes! Which must mean they were raised by a pack of lesbos, right? Wrong, actually, further analysis inquiries showed that only 2 of the trolls were supposedly raised by lesbians. None of the people were really parented by gays or lesbians. But, in Christian sociology bad data, worse measures, and perfunctory analyses are SCIENCE god damn it, and Marky Mark will be in Illinois telling his little buddies that he proved that gays and lesbians are evil parents! Praise the lord.

Indeed, sociology has been a closet full of Christians teaching sociology since before Karl Marx kicked the bucket. And what, pray tell, do Christian Sociologists do? Well, they blame the poors and the browns and the women and the homosexualists and the commies for all of our "social problems." Duh! They've been doing this shit since the 1880s! Fortunately for you, most of the Christian Sociologists have historically taught at Christianist Bible Colleges instead of your good liberal communist universities. Unfortunately, history has a way of changing, and not always for the better. With the advance of university education after the commies got to outer space first, bible college seemed a bit lame. First, the christianists renamed their bible colleges "universities," only that didn't really seem to help much. Then, a few devious christianists decided to infiltrate higher education and destroy it from within. So, they got all smart acting and kept their bibles locked in their closets. And the rich christianists who made money off of farm subsidies, oil, and the military industrial complex donated money to lure the best and the brightest christianist children to college and grandcollege to become "idea creators" and to combat the evil ideas of equality, democracy, feminism, non-brown-hating, and shit like that. And, boy, were we surprised! While the rest of us lived on non-vegan inorganic peanut butter and jelly and drank PBR when it was not at all hip and worked extra jobs as sex workers and waitrixes and library serfs, the Christianists had real apartments and paid their rent and could go to conferences and stay at hotels and not have to share the bathtub with four other people and get paid year round by their "fellowships." Of course, that was only the Christianists with penises, the non-penised christianists had to birth lots of babies and serve their limp patriarchs.

The Christian sociologists got all kinds of monies to do "research" even when they were lowly graduate students—some of them had six figure grants, because Science=Jesus=Fuck-you-women-homos-poors-hippies-and-browns. Back in the old days when Bill Clinton was not really having very good sex for Monica Lewinsky, the christianists remained in the closet, so us communist atheist homosexualist sociologists thought they were just like those weird-but-harmless jesus freaks who took too much acid. I remember one time when I couldn't get tickets to Rage Against the Machine during the real sociology meetings I even bought a gaggle of them shots of good tequila at a Messican restaurant in NYC (well, not really, the nice waitrix who liked me bought us a round . . .). Surely they were nice guys with funny haircuts and housewives, right? NUH UH! After Al Gore was elected president and kicked out of office the "evangelicals" became "emboldened" and as each one of them made tenure at their public universities they came out of the closet and said things like "feminists are the source of all evil" and "women are whores who hate sex and make good women sad and turn men into homos" and "gays and lesbians are bad parents who molest their children to make them into homosexicans too, also."

Unfortunately for me, that last one wound up causing me all sorts of problems, threats of lawsuits from right wing foundations, whore marketing firms, and even harassment from LGBT persons who never quite got the memo about who the bad guys were. Ah well, such is "scholarship," where the defenders of heterosexuality boldly claim patriarchal superiority while appearing in sissy looking glamour shots with their Ted Haggard haircuts, and the poor Iranianredneck (oh, right, me) fights on in his manly spandex. But just remember when you can't sleep at night that they are out there. Christian sociologists with millions of dollars doing research to you to prove that you suck and should be locked up and have your children taken away or be forced to have children if you don't have any and get married to a man if you are a lady even if you don't like penis and not get married to a man if you do like penis and have one. They even want to close down sperm banks so lesbo-americans and women who are not owned by a penis cannot make babies! What will they do with all that sperm? I do not know.[32]

This is only one among other similar blog posts offering this sociologist's extra-institutional, public "evaluation" of his professional colleagues.[33] This is no lunatic-fringe scholar, but a well-published sociologist and member in good standing of the ASA and two other sociology associations, the previous co-editor of a sociology-of-religion journal, a consulting editor for eight outstanding sociology journals, and the reviewer of submitted articles, book manuscripts, and grant proposals for 64 different journals, publishers, and funding agencies (according to his curriculum vitae).

Now, anyone may wish to defend (or not) this person's free-speech right to publish such blog posts. That is not my concern here. The question for sociology as a discipline is how such publications by sociologists on the Internet affect the institutionalized peer-review process. The same question applies to other blog posts like them with the same intent and practical effect but conveyed in more "professional" language and actually argued with some evidence. Despite the official double-blind character of journal reviews, many authors and reviewers often think that they can accurately guess—based on article content, citation patterns, and tone of writing, and sometimes accurately so, I think—who the paper authors and peer reviewers are with whom they are dealing. So what does it do to the credibility of the peer-review system when sociologists involved believe or know that the colleagues who are reviewing their papers are the same people who are also publishing the above kind of posts

32. http://wonkette.com/518227/lets-all-laugh-at-the-christianist-sociologists-with-an-actual-sociologist-who-is-not-dumb.
33. Most of which are found on this author's personal weblog, complete with rampant obscenity and pictures of animals trying to copulate with other dead animals and with statues of animals of different species (as of June 6, 2013).

on Internet blogs? Can their paper reviews be assumed to be fair, even-handed, unbiased? Having spewed the above kinds of middle-schoolish vitriol, can such colleagues be assumed and trusted to engage the scholarly review process as true "professionals?"

As I said above, the ASA's professional-ethics people seem to have not even begun to think about how to handle the destructive potential of sociologists posting about other sociologists and their work on the Internet. Its official Code of Ethics is so far behind the curve (essentially in the 1980s) in being capable of addressing such matters that it's not funny. The more focused point for present purposes that all sociologists need to grapple with, however, is simply that the Internet has created new means by which American sociology's spiritual project—especially in its more sectarian and activist forms—can and does interfere with the integrity and trustworthiness of the social-scientific, journal article peer-review system. The very possibility of sustaining this essential mechanism for ensuring the reliability of published social science requires a searching reflection on the reality and influence of that sacred project.

ALIENATED SOCIOLOGISTS

American sociology has lost some very good scholars from its ranks because the exclusive narrowness of its sacred vision has driven them away. True believers in the sacred project might say, "good riddance to them," but I think that is mistaken. Such out-selection processes of exclusion only work to further narrow vision and thinking among sociologists, which cannot be good for the long-term health of the discipline. I think, for example, of Peter Berger—undeniably a major sociological theorist who actually did more than anyone to originally develop the social constructionist perspective that has become so crucial to sociology's spiritual project. In fact, his book

The Social Construction of Reality has been named by the International Sociological Association as the fifth most important book in sociology published in the twentieth century.[34] In the late 1960s and the 1970s, however, Berger began to reconsider and question some of what he viewed as the leftist dogma dominating his discipline, especially as it addressed questions of global socioeconomic development. That led to what he describes as an "exile" from mainstream American sociology.[35]

As to good sociologists whom the mainstream discipline has lost as active interlocutors, I think too of James D. Hunter—another critical intellectual whose analyses of culture have something important to contribute to the larger discussions, yet who has also become alienated from the mainstream sociological profession. In some ways, I think Hunter was simply too theoretically perceptive to find conventional sociology interesting—and in that sense was perhaps doomed to alienation from ASA-style sociology from the start. But the crucial turn happened, I think, with the publication of his book *Culture Wars*, which was highly influential outside of sociology but criticized within (including by me). I think the book did have some actual flaws, but they do not fully explain its poor reception in sociology. In part I think its popular acclaim evoked a kind of sour-grapes envy on the part of some colleagues who resented the attention and books sales it gave to Hunter. I suspect more than a few felt, "Why doesn't the world pay as much attention to *my* work, which is better sociology?" Some dismissively described Hunter to me as "a popularizer"—an epitaph of derision reserved for someone who is not a "real" sociologist but who plays to the public with thin scholarship.[36]

---

34. http://www.isa-sociology.org/books/books10.htm.

35. Peter Berger, 2011, *Adventures of an Accidental Sociologist*, Amherst, NY: Prometheus Books, pp. 104 ff.

36. See Jonathan Imber, 2005, "Ambition, Vocation, and Sociology," *The American Sociologist*, Summer, pp. 76–85.

More importantly for my argument here, however, is the fact that Hunter's culture-wars thesis threw wrenches into the gears of sociology's sacred project. For one thing, it claimed that cultural and political activists are motivated not so much by material interests or the obvious demands of justice but by deeply held "progressive" and "traditionalist" worldview beliefs about ultimate truth and authority. If that is true, it exposes the genuinely spiritual and contingent nature of the progressive project to which most American sociologists are committed, but which is to them, as I have suggested above, just obvious and invisible. So, Hunter's was a suggestion that hit too close to home for comfort. Hunter's book also plainly stated the extent to which academics, intellectuals, and many knowledge-class professionals, like sociologists, are outright *activists*, in the pursuit of what I am calling their sacred project, engaged in social and political movements for cultural transformation driven by spiritual visions and ends. That, too, was a too-candid description that could not be allowed to stick. And, if Hunter's story was right about the general nature and contours of the cultural divisions, then it would mean that the claims of traditionalists and conservatives are understandable in the American experience and politically legitimate (whether or not they are healthy, good or right), such that sociologists would have to take "those people" seriously even if they find them detestable. That too was unacceptable. So Hunter's book was taken apart, and only somewhat fairly so. Since then, Hunter has largely (and, to me, understandably) turned his back on mainstream sociology and is running his own independent Institute for Advanced Studies in Culture at the University of Virginia. The latter fosters really interesting and important big-picture discussions and scholarship (which mainstream sociology mostly ignores). I understand why Hunter has opted for that route as an alienated intellectual, but in my view it is a loss intellectually for mainstream American sociology.

We can think of other similar examples. Another in my own field of sociology of religion is Jose Casanova, a superbly interesting, cosmopolitan sociologist-intellectual who also decided that mainstream American sociology is a boringly parochial lost cause and so who prefers to spend his time and energy in big-picture, interdisciplinary discussions taking place around the globe. Casanova can be found in interesting seminars and workshops in Kiev, Istanbul, and Johannesburg, but he is rarely seen in the halls of ASA meetings. And his disconnect from the center of American sociology is, like Berger and Hunter's, most certainly a genuine intellectual loss for the discipline, which I, for one, lament. I could continue to run down a list of similarly alienated sociologists who, for one reason or another—despite their love for the essential discipline of sociology—cannot stomach the attitude, standards, and practices of mainstream American sociology as a profession, most of which are defined and driven one way or another by its unacknowledged sacred project. Suffice it for now, however, to offer these three examples and to move on. The essential point here I have either made convincingly or never will.

SELF AS BLIND SPOT

One way to summarize my argument is to say that not many sociologists are as sociological about themselves as they are about the world around them. They can carefully train their sociological scopes on everyone and everything beyond themselves, yet fail to see and name the basic true character of the project that animates and directs their own professional endeavors. That may be disappointing—it is to me—but it is not very surprising. Sociologists, after all, are only ordinary humans. And we know that humans are very good at pointing out the specks in the eyes of other people and ignoring the planks lodged in our own eyes. Still, one might hope that sociologists could be more honestly sociological about themselves. Unfortunately, one of the apparent characteristics of the sacred project I named above is that its very *obvious rightness* in the eyes of those committed to it tends to make it invisible to its disciples. For them, it is just self-evident *reality*. The only need, then, for any sociological analysis or debunking is to expose for transformation anything outside of sociology that gets in the way of realizing the sacred aspirations of that project. That and only that is what the critical sociological eye is meant for. And that explains why and how American sociology operates with highly selective criticism as it does today and proves to be so conservative when it comes to itself as a discipline.

Chapter 6

The Question of Accountability

What I have said above raises the uncomfortable and potentially dangerous but nonetheless important question of accountability. To whom, if anyone, is American sociology accountable? To whom does it have to give an explanation for the resources it consumes, the value it produces with them, and the effects it has on the world? I am not implying that sociology is a waste of resources that should be shut down. Absolutely not. A world like ours lacking in any kind of sociology would be greatly diminished, I believe. But the legitimate question remains: To whom is sociology accountable? As far as I can discern, not much to anyone at all. The way academia currently works, most of sociology can carry on as it pleases, under its own direction and oversight—confidently championing its sacred project and whatever else it wishes—without having to explain or justify itself to anyone with any authority to ask difficult questions, demand good answers, and enforce consequences.

A mind experiment: Imagine that all colleges and universities operated all of their undergraduate course enrollments as pure markets (an idea I oppose), rather than partly governed to fulfill core requirements. Sociology would then have to prove its appeal and worth with students by competing for them to register in sociology courses instead of other classes. What would happen? I think a reasonable number of undergraduate students—mostly those who are already inclined to embrace its sacred project—would enroll in some sociology courses even if they had absolute freedom of choice among all courses. Overall sociology enrollments, however, would probably decline. But few sociology departments today actually have to worry about that, since the divisional distributions of most core course curricula require most college students to take at least one basic social science course. So, most sociology departments benefit from the fact that some percentage of all students is being forced to take their courses (assuming that some, given this forced choice, will prefer sociology over economics or political science). In principle I think sociology faculty should therefore be thus bound by some level of accountability to their undergraduate students. But in practice that almost always concerns the fairness of grading, not the value of sociology itself or the legitimacy of its sacred project.

American sociology faculty are also accountable to some degree to their department chair, formally, at least. But to chairs they are largely accountable for teaching their classes decently, for not violating institutional standards of conduct, for serving on an adequate number of committees, and for researching and publishing enough to merit tenure and promotion (and hopefully not being too embarrassing in their lack of productivity after tenure and promotion). Extremely rarely do any members of any sociology faculty have to account to anyone for the ideological, political, or spiritual (as long as it is secular) content of what they teach in their classes. That would be seen as a gross violation of academic freedom, intellectual autonomy, and creative expression. The number of sociology department chairs who are prepared to engage their faculty on the issues I am raising here are scarce as hen's teeth. Much more powerful motives and concerns for most department chairs are to not rock the boat, to not have any major controversies, and to come out somewhat stronger as a department than when they took over the position. So we find not much accountability there either.

The faculty of American sociology departments are also formally accountable to their Deans, but that typically happens indirectly through department chairs, who are usually able when they wish to act as buffers between those higher authorities and anything questionable happening in their departments. In any case, most academic Deans are products of the same academic system that sustains sociology in its current form, do not know enough about the bigger-picture issues I am raising here to even be capable of inquiring about them, and are primarily interested in stability and gradual improvement on matters of institutional metrics. They do not want anything explosive or divisive happening on their watch, so the asking of difficult, controversial questions is usually out—instead, the building of consensus, the overseeing of mild reforms, and the shepherding of specific initiatives are as far as most Deans are likely to venture. What I have just observed of Deans applies equally to most Provosts—and don't even ask about college and university Boards of Trustees. In the end, as long as sociology faculty members are not having affairs with students, not neglecting their most minimal of duties, and not otherwise creating havoc or embarrassment, few Deans or Provosts are going to hold them seriously accountable for anything else that might create controversy.

Accountability of sociologists to their students' parents for what sociology is ultimately about and how that is expressed in classrooms and beyond is even less likely. The same dynamics described above pertain to parents, only more so. Those few parents who might ask difficult questions about the sociology their sons or daughters are studying would likely be viewed by faculty as "helicopter" parents inappropriately meddling in their children's school affairs and so preventing them from becoming autonomous, self-directing adults. In any case, almost no parent of any sociology student ever asks such penetrating questions. The main question from any parents that sociologists ever have to answer is, "What practically is my daughter ever going to be able to do with a sociology major?" It is the material self-sufficiency of their children, not the spirituality of sociology, that students' parents have on their minds.

Even supposing, however, that some brave, smart parents began asking difficult questions about the implicit spiritual-ideological-political-moral project into which sociology is socializing their children, under the cover of being a "science of society," they would one way or another be deflected and disempowered by those invested in the sacred project. What do ordinary parents know about such higher truths?, sociologists would ask. Those kinds of people are mostly "conservatives" who do not appreciate the liberalizing that education produces and for which universities are set up to achieve in the first place, they would say. So sociology is simply not accountable to the families that entrust their children into its hands and who often sacrifice to pay the tuition for the privilege. The most authority that any parents have in dealing with the kind of issues I raise here is simply to persuade or force their son or daughter to take different classes or switch to a different major—in brief, to find an individualistic solution to their seemingly personal problem, rather than a systemic solution to a possible institutional problem.

What about state legislatures in the case of public colleges and universities? Is American sociology accountable to them for the inestimable citizens' tax dollars they appropriate in budgets to sustain public colleges and universities and the sociology departments within them? Of course not—nor, in my view, should they be. Sociologists have their Deans, Provosts, Presidents, and members of their Boards of Trustees to answer to state legislatures for their larger contributions or lack thereof to the public good, and if that kind of accountability system is not working now, then asking sociologists to somehow be directly accountable to legislators would work even worse. My view is that, in principle, everyone in academia should be accountable *in some significant ways* to—though certainly not controlled by—the tax-paying citizens and their political representatives who directly and indirectly support nearly everyone in American higher education. Academics simply should not be able to directly and indirectly take large amounts of money from state and federal governments and then hold themselves above accountability for what goods (or bads) they are or are not accomplishing with those resources. However, elected members of political legislatures are *not* the people to manage that kind of accountability, much less control university education. They would not know what they are doing and would only make more problems—perhaps not unlike the oppressive bureaucratic accountability system the Margaret Thatcher administration (ironically, given its opposition to state bureaucracy) created, which still plagues higher education in Britain. So, let us remove political legislators from the list of those to whom sociology might be accountable.

To whom else might sociology be accountable for its sacred project? The faculty of other social science departments? No way. Social science departments are self-contained units sponsoring very different disciplinary projects and identities, and exist in mutual competition for fixed pools of college resources, the faculty of which are therefore not about to submit in any kind of accountability to each other. In fact, it is the job of Deans today to keep different departments operating on parallel tracks, not getting into struggles over control of turf and related conflicts, however intellectually important and interesting. Then how about accountable to generous financial donors to colleges and universities (who actually may collectively possess the power to make real internal changes in colleges and universities)? Don't even think about it. They are handled by professional college and university development offices, whose job it is to convey nothing but good news about everything that is happening or could be happening (with more money) on campus. Well then, might sociology be accountable to "society?" Silly. "Society" is a conceptual abstraction. Nobody is accountable to conceptual abstractions. So the list of realistic possibilities here grows short.

Sociologists are accountable to other sociologists in at least some ways. Sociologists read and evaluate each other's papers and book manuscripts in processes of peer review for publication, for example. Sociologists serve on external review committees to periodically visit and review other sociology departments. Sociologists make up the research, teaching, and service committees that review the records of junior-faculty colleagues going up for tenure and promotion and of associate professors seeking promotion to full professor. Sociologists routinely give talks and presentations at their own and other sociology departments, in which they are accountable to provide satisfactory answers to questions. They write reviews of their colleagues' books. They fill out surveys that help rank each other's graduate departments in reputational systems. They write external review letters for colleagues in other departments who are being considered for promotion. Sociologists review and evaluate the research proposals that other sociologists submit to funding agencies. They write letters of recommendation for student sociologists and sometimes other colleagues who are seeking internships and jobs. And sociologists sit on official committees and panels whose jobs it is to formulate codes of ethics, editorial guidelines, and other discipline-defining standards. In short, sociologists are quite accountable to and for other sociologists in many ways. And this is as it should be, in my view—at least when a discipline is diverse and healthy enough to monitor, question, and amend itself when necessary.

The question to ask, however—in light of all I have observed above—is whether American sociology is actually diverse and healthy enough where it really counts to recognize, acknowledge, and fairly evaluate its own sacred project for what it really is. If my argument above is correct, the answer is "no." Asking sociologists to seriously and critically consider the merits and appropriateness of their own discipline's sacred project would be futile. It would not be quite like asking the fox to guard the henhouse, rather more like asking the hens to guard the henhouse—and to be in charge of doling out the chicken feed while they're at it. Few sociologists would even have the perspective to know exactly what they were guarding, but would be more than happy to dole out the feed. For sociologists to successfully evaluate their own sacred project would require a great deal more internal spiritual, ideological, and political diversity than currently exists; a genuine readiness to listen carefully to and consider critical voices expressing doubts and critiques of things taken for granted; institutional mechanisms by which to sustain open, honest, and fair debates and discussions across different perspectives; and the epistemological humility all around to remain open to the possibility of being wrong. Those conditions no more obtain in American sociology today than they do in any henhouse. It is simply not going to happen anytime soon.

And so, in my wonderings about accountability, I am left at an impasse. American sociology is a sacred project that deserves some careful scrutiny. But sociology stands in no relation of accountability to anyone who might foster such scrutiny in an open, fair, and constructive way. And so, American sociology's sacred project continues freely and without accountability to be promoted and reproduced—an invisible, misrecognized, unevaluated endeavor operating under the banner of the "study of society" to potently determine the discipline's driving interests, character, results, and self-reproduction.

Chapter 7

What Is Sociology Good For?

There are days when I am tempted to think that sociology as an enterprise should simply be shut down; that the loss in value to the world by its disappearance would be offset by the elimination of some of its more distorting, sometimes pernicious, effects in higher education and beyond; and that the resources spent on it could be better used elsewhere. But I never think that for long. I always come back to believing that sociology, warts and all, does make a unique and important contribution to the common good, that if sociology simply disappeared, something truly valuable (not just sociologists' careers) would be lost. However, I also think that sociology could make a more valuable contribution than it does now if some of its warts were removed. There are other days when I think sociology maybe should be downsized to a more modest discipline of "sociography," to focus and capitalize upon the part of its work that it tends to be quite good at already: using its empirical research methods simply to describe the contours of the social world as accurately as possible. Then a broad array of actors and interpreters in society could sort the normative social and political implications of what those facts mean and what should be done about them.

This would restrain some of the license that sociologists currently have to impose on their data their own preferred visions, ideologies, agendas, politics, and values under the guise of "theory" and "interpretation."

But I also never remain satisfied with the idea of downscaling the discipline to a mere "sociography" of this sort. Accurate *description* is terrifically important, but insufficient. The proper task of sociology (or whatever else we might call it) also entails *understanding* and *explaining* human social life, not merely describing it. And that requires the difficult theoretical task of identifying and theoretically describing the combinations of causal social mechanisms that operate in intricately interactive ways in complex contexts across temporal sequences to produce outcomes and states of affairs that are interesting and important for human persons. Sociology at its best really is a science—though one most effectively framed by the philosophy of critical realism, not positivist empiricism. We cannot do without reality-appropriate concepts, accounts of causal mechanisms, and theoretical frameworks that enable us to understand and explain the social world. So, *something like* sociology as it has been received, conceived, and practiced is valuable and necessary (and worth reforming), and into which significant resources are worth investing, I think. The question is, how would a better version of sociology be like and unlike what we have today?

I will not tinker here with specifics. Before getting to that point, what is most needed, in my view, is a bigger-picture conceptual view of what sociology is good for, after which we can ponder more specific implications. In my view, social science's greatest contribution to the societies that sustain it with resources is simply *reporting back to those societies what really is going on in and among them, why and how so, and with what apparent consequences.* That is the service of social self-reflexivity that is so valuable when performed well, a service well worthy of the resources invested in it. That requires describing the world accurately, but also understanding and explaining it well to people outside of social science.[1]

This approach understands sociology not as an autonomous, self-serving academic niche deserved by those who manage to find a tenured place in it—not to mention a safe haven for semi-covert, sacred ideological-political-moral movements and campaigns to transform culture and society often against its will, rather than through shared deliberative civil-society and democratic processes. My proposed approach instead understands sociology as ultimately a society-serving discipline that is commissioned by and accountable to the larger social orders that support it. Sociology's job in this view is to do its very best to tell the truth about what is happening in society, what is causing it, and what consequences seem to be produced as a result. This view gives sociology two key tasks: reporting and explaining, the purpose of which is to promote public understanding and self-reflection. Greater public understanding should then be fed into the many deliberative and self-reflexive processes of self-understanding that operate in any healthy society, from discussions around the family dinner table to fruitful debates within various kinds of social institutions to widespread citizen participation in processes of political decision making.

In my view, then, sociology at its best expands and enriches human personal and social self-understanding by reflecting upon, reporting about, and explaining the what's, why's, and how's of human experience, institutions, and practices and, as a result, making better sense of them for the variety of people and groups

1. This is what I have attempted to do in my recent books, including, for example, Christian Smith, Kari Christoffersen, Hilary Davidson, and Patricia Snell Herzog, 2011, *Lost in Transition: The Dark Side of Emerging Adulthood*, New York: Oxford University Press, which presents its normative commitments explicitly (pp. 8–11).

involved. Human experience is real, even if not self-interpreting, and can be highly informative when reflected upon well. Sociology can do a lot of great value to foster that. Human self-understanding is thus enhanced through the conceptually mediated, reasoned, theoretical comprehension of ourselves and our world, viewed through sociological lenses, in response to our personal and collective experiences over time. When sociology accomplishes that, I believe its contribution is invaluable.

Sociology serving this public role is quite different from activist sociologists using the discipline to push their spiritually driven program of cultural and social transformation. The crucial difference is between sociology as a promoter of human self-understanding in all of its complexity versus sociology as a promoter of a particular agenda concerning a specific idea about good human lives and society. The first requires openness, curiosity, humility, versatility, pluralism, and the ability to relate to a host of different kinds of people and groups. The second requires an ideological package, self-assurance, superiority, zeal, a readiness to take out rivals, and a knack for proselytizing others. I have no doubt that contemporary American sociology as a collective enterprise—whichever of the first set of virtues it might or might not have at one time embodied—has drifted increasingly into an approach to the world that much more reflects the second set of features. And that, I suggest, is not good for students, higher education, the society that underwrites sociology, and ultimately the discipline of sociology itself.

The problem with my view of sociology as reporting back to those societies that support it what really is going on in and among them, why and how so, and with what apparent consequences—and then allowing the many deliberative functions of those societies to determine what to do about it—is that the disciples of sociology's sacred project do not trust ordinary people and social institutions to know the "right" things to do or to actually do them. In fact, in sociology's dominant view, it is ordinary people and institutions that are a main part of the problem with the world. Therefore, sociology as a discipline—the movement of enlightened ones—needs to act as the vanguard to push people and society, to become activists in protest, to agitate, to mobilize, to force people to do the "right" thing.

Chapter 8

Conclusion

American sociology is not simply the science of society nor merely a politically liberal-leaning discipline, but a particular sacred project, a movement to venerate, protect, and advance a specific Durkheimian sacred. That project is to realize the emancipation, equality, and moral affirmation of all human beings as autonomous, self-directing, individual agents (who should be) out to live their lives as they personally so desire. And that compels sociology to work to expose, protest, and end through social movements and state regulations and programs all human inequality, oppression, exploitation, suffering, injustice, poverty, discrimination, exclusion, hierarchy, and constraint of, by, and over other humans. I have presented a range of empirical evidence representing important aspects of American sociology to support this claim. I have suggested that a significant minority of American sociologists pursue this sacred project with all the zeal of new religious converts. A majority of other sociologists essentially support its vision as their background outlook, though are more measured in their promotion of it, yet seem content to go along with their more zealous colleagues in most ways. Only a small minority of miscellaneous other types of sociologists, who believe in what seems to be a less normative scientific version of sociology or some other different vision, are resistant to the sacred project that dominates their discipline. They, however, have relatively little impact when it comes to opposing or supporting this project.

I sketched out a historical account to indicate how American sociology got to this particular place. I also explored a number of ways that I believe sociology's sacred project limits and corrodes sociology's proper disciplinary mission. Carrying on the spiritual project, I suggested, requires dishonesty about the discipline; generates difficult tensions and contradictions within sociology; fosters a counterproductive, standardized, nonpluralistic, uniform orthodoxy among sociologists; puts blinkers and filters on sociologists' capacity to see the world accurately and make sense of it optimally; threatens to corrupt the integrity of the scientific peer-review process; and alienates some sociologists whose thoughts and voices if included would benefit sociology. Having explored these problems, I then observed that sociologists stand in few relationships of accountability to anyone but themselves, which—given the dominance of the sacred project—does not position sociology well to be self-critical or interested in internal change.

I must stress again before ending that it would be incomplete and inaccurate for readers to insist that sociology's project is essentially only "political." Observers recurrently note and sometimes criticize sociologists as a group for being strongly liberal-leaning if not outright leftists. Those observations are often generally true, but they do not get to the heart of the matter I raise here. All people are political in one way or another—even when they think and behave in ways that seem apolitical. In the United States, there is in principle nothing more problematic about being a leftist than a centrist, conservative, libertarian, or most anything else. In a healthy system of higher education, it is necessary that students and others confront and work through a variety of different perspectives and arguments in the often-difficult search for what is true—or at least so I believe. So my interest here is not that American sociologists are liberal or leftist per se. The issue is bigger than that. Nor is my concern simply that American sociology is pursuing a *spiritual* project, as if any project that is spiritual is per se suspect or bad. I think most human beings are—whether they know or admit it or not—engaged in the pursuit of some sacred project or other (for an alternative project that I find compelling, see the Appendix). Concerns with matters sacred, as I described that above, are an inevitable part of the human condition, insofar as the "human spirit" helps constitute human personhood. So sociologists, and everybody else for that matter, not only may pursue sacred projects but inevitably do and will. My issue here is not the sacred nature of American sociology's project per se. My point, rather, is to make an observation that I think is rarely recognized and understood. And to make that point clearly, it is necessary to say that the "sacred project" of sociology cannot be described or evaluated as simply the idea of "improving human well-being" or its having political commitments.

What I am describing here is much bigger, deeper, and more meaningful, profound, and ultimate than being merely a political, ideological, or moral matter. At stake in American sociology's project are a vision and a cause expressing what are believed to be the greatest, highest, most authentic goods, truths, values, meanings, and purposes. In question are fundamental and ultimate issues of human existence, experience, feeling, and desire. This is a Durkheimian sacred. Mobilizing sociologists in the struggle on behalf of the project is a dedication of the human spirit to what is believed to be most worthy of one's devotion, true goods to be cherished, and purposes justifying a life's investment and dedication. At issue are not merely the material and instrumental affairs of human life that much of politics and ideology engage, but rather concerns and ideals drawn from the deepest wellsprings of people's hearts. Because in these ways sociology's project engages what is believed to be a noble moral cause of weighty human meaning, ultimate value, and world-historical consequence defining the ultimate horizons of vision, purpose, and devotion, we can and ought to call the project of American sociology sacred and spiritual and not merely political or moral or ideological or scientific. So where does that leave us?

American sociology now faces a choice: It can either play dumb or come clean. The first option would try to take the position of denial and ignorance, expressed in one of two forms. The first form would say, "What are you talking about? We in sociology have no sacred, normative, ideological, moral, political vision and aspirations. We are simply the science of society that produces empirical facts and rational analyses." That approach would amount to outright lying, or at least self-delusion. The second form of denial and ignorance would instead have to say something like, "Yes, we have a sacred project, but it is obviously the only morally defensible commitment available—there's no use thinking much about it, since there aren't any other options." Saying that would be less deceptive but would reveal a sadly parochial lack of imagination and knowledge that would not build anyone's respect for sociology as a discipline. If sociologists really think that their own sacred project is the only morally viable option available, then we are even more sectarian and zealously myopic than I had imagined.

The alternative, second approach of coming clean would require American sociologists to say, publicly and frankly, "Yes, this is our project and, yes, it is driven by the deepest depths of our human spirits. And, yes, we believe this is the right way to understand life and the world that everyone else should embrace and follow. And, yes, we think it is legitimate to pursue and promote this sacred project as and in our academic discipline, relying on the money of tuition-paying students and their families, taxpayer dollars, and donations of alumni and friends of our colleges and universities.

We believe that this position and our commitment are absolutely just and defensible, and are prepared to reasonably debate in public anyone who thinks otherwise." That would be the high road for sociology to take, the course which I encourage, for starters, at least. Such an approach would at minimum have the virtues of being honest and clear. It would foster a more candid accounting within sociology of our purposes, tensions, vulnerabilities, and the sacred project's more problematic side.[1] And, as the discussions would work themselves out, it would have the felicitous consequence over time, I believe, in improving the value and importance of sociology's contribution to its students and the world beyond academia.

Is it possible that we in sociology might head in such a direction? I hope so, yet I am not optimistic. So how, realistically, is the argument of this book likely be received? One of the less-impressive features of many American sociologists who are most caught up in the discipline's sacred project is how predictable they are in so many ways. Although I am hopeful that many sociologists who read this book will take its argument to heart, enhance their self-understanding, and consider alternative approaches, I am not naïve enough to expect that I will win over most of those already converted to sociology's sacred project. If this book gets any play, it will make at least some of them uncomfortable, perhaps even angry. Highly predictable will then be the reaction that this book will evoke.

Here will be the game plan, if I am not mistaken, for those sociologists who are the true believers in the sacred project. They will dismiss my idea of sociology having anything to do with "spiritual" as preposterous on the face of it, though without actually replying to my description of, argument about, and examples substantiating

---

1 Sociology needs many such candid discussions about a variety of issues—see, for example, Nicholas Christakis, 2013, "Let's Shake Up the Social Sciences," *New York Times Sunday Review* (July 19), http://www.nytimes.com/2013/07/21/opinion/sunday/lets-shake-up-the-social-sciences.html?hp&_r=0.

it. They will accuse me of "cherry-picking" my evidence to fit my story and of setting up a "straw man" to knock down, all the while ignoring my actual evidence and arguments. They will accuse me of being "a conservative"—that being in and of itself a damning label for the relevant crowds here, the slapping on of which automatically makes the slapped one utterly dismissible—even though I am in fact not a conservative, but a personalist, which actually makes more than a few of my views more radical than those the American liberal-progressive-lefty program typically offers up (unfortunately, American liberal-progressive-lefty types find it nearly impossible to conceive of principled philosophical commitments that do not easily line up on the tediously shopworn conservative-liberal-radical political spectrum). I will be denounced for being irredeemably biased by either my personal religious commitments (always a good discrediting fact to mention with tones of ominous insinuation) or the research grant money that I have received from various private foundations (yes, their Directors of Ideology really do get together and push me around behind closed doors so that I obsequiously do their normative bidding—unlike every other funding agency, which have no normative interests whatsoever). Some will email me (just as happened before when I wrote my piece in the *Chronicle* about the Regnerus disaster) literally demanding that I publicly repent and "apologize to the discipline" for writing such hurtful and untrue things—another version of *"You have betrayed us!"* Some less level-headed colleagues may file formal charges of professional misconduct with my university and the ASA (indicating their basic lack of understanding of what "professional misconduct" is). If none of that works—or even if it does—some additional *ad hominem* criticisms may come in handy. To be most effective, some sociologist colleague(s) happy to do the dirty work will need to feed this (mis)information to certain "journalists," who will then add errors and distortions and disseminate it to particular segmented audiences through various unanswerable channels on the Internet and beyond. Based on previous experiences in recent events, at least, that is what we can expect to happen.

The larger proportion of American sociologists who are not true believers but are nonetheless tacitly friendly to the discipline's sacred project will, on the other hand, respond in generally more reasonable ways. Many of these will acknowledge parts of the truth of what I say here, but will suggest that it applies only to a small minority of sociologists on the fringe of the discipline, who do not represent them or their interests at all—thus attempting to contain my argument by claiming that, yes, I am onto something real here but am blowing it out of proportion. Others will agree with some of my characterizations of types of colleagues in political terms, but will remain confused and unconvinced about the "spiritual project" idea. Others will not deny much of what I am saying, even its deeply sacred character, but will most of all worry pragmatically whether my saying it in print will hurt institutional and research funding for sociology, thus essentially ignoring the substantive issues I raise by focusing on practical material consequences (as if the issues I raise do not actually have their own profound long-term practical material consequences). Some may complain that my attitude is "arrogant"—as if that, even if it were true, has anything to do with what matters here. Still others will simply wonder why I am being so cranky, why I cannot leave well enough alone. Why air all the dirty laundry? Many will have little to say, but will privately wonder how and why it could be that I am not a straight supporter of sociology's sacred project. I sincerely hope that my colleagues respond to this book more openly and thoughtfully. Perhaps they will. I believe that much of importance depends upon it.

In my observations, many sociologists (and no doubt other academics, although, again, I am not concerned with them here) behave as if they believe (ironically, given their belief in social constructionism) that robust institutions of higher education are an automatic and natural feature of any conceivable society, that nice and secure academic jobs are something like a civil right guaranteed for those who have passed the hurdles to have landed them, and that the American public owes it to academics like themselves to provide the necessary resources to continue indefinitely to do their jobs as they have done them in the past. The underlying attitude is almost as if sociology is God's gift to society, and so must be and definitely will be sustained with the required resources. Few sociologists in my observation seem aware of how brief American sociology's history has been, how unsuccessful sociology has been in achieving most of its early promises, and how serious and widespread current public discussions are about the value, condition, and possible alternative deliveries of higher education in the United States.[2] Many of the assumptions behind those discussions I am convinced are badly confused, though some of the arguments made are also reasonable.

But sociologists' possible delusions about the matter do not change the fact that such serious reconsiderations of higher education are happening now and could culminate in some drastic changes for college and university faculty. Meanwhile, most faculty members in disciplines like sociology continue in their academic Versailles to pursue business as usual, imagining that if the rabble

---

2 See, among the burgeoning literature, for example, Richard Arum and Josipa Roksa, 2010, *Academically Adrift: Limited Learning on College Campuses*, Chicago: University of Chicago Press; Anthony Kronman, 2008, *Education's End: Why our Colleges and Universities Have Given Up on the Meaning of Life*, New Haven: Yale University Press; Harry Lewis, 2007, *Excellent Without a Soul: Does Liberal Education Have a Future?*, New York: Public Affairs; Jeffrey Selingo, 2013, *College Unbound: The Future of Higher Education and What It Means for Students*, New York: New Harvest; Victor Ferrall, 2011, *Liberal Arts at the Brink*, Cambridge: Harvard University Press; Richard Schwartz, 2012, *Is a College Education Still Worth the Price? A Dean's Sobering Perspective*, Los Angeles: Now and Then Reader; William Bennett, 2013, *Is College Worth It?*, Nashville: Thomas Nelson; Glenn Reynolds, 2012, *The Higher Education Bubble*, New York: Encounter Books; http://www.newcriterion.com/articles.cfm/Higher-education-bubble--Williams-edition-7651.

outside the walls of their islands of enlightenment threaten their received ways of life, then they can simply eat cake. Such threats can also be sociologized away with smart analyses of political and corporate ignorance and other social problems, and the resulting snappy books written about that can be displayed in future ASA book exhibits. But increasingly such responses simply amount to putting our sociological heads in the proverbial sand.[3] Sociology continuing tenaciously to pursue its sacred project, even while living in denial about the fact that it actually is and has such a project, will not foster a bright future for the discipline, given the kind of problematic and sometimes destructive consequences caused by that project. Sociology needs to do some serious, truly open-minded soul searching about its proper purpose, identity, and practices before it loses what is genuinely good in what is has to offer.

---

3 It never ceases to amaze me how many sociological colleagues, the same who are so determined to change the world "out there," can become so conservative and resistant to any possible threats of change when it comes to our own discipline, practices, and relatively comfortable ways of life in academia.

The Alternative of Critical Realist Personalism

Many American sociologists will not only find it impossible to see the sacred project that sociology is—precisely because my argument above is correct—but they will also be unable to imagine any realistic alternatives. How else, they will wonder, can one be a well-educated, morally astute, politically engaged, world-transforming person and scholar if not by embracing and promoting the sacred project in question? Again, the lack of imagination and education here is evident. There is definitely at least one good alternative sacred project to the one that dominates American sociology. That vision is defined by critical realist personalism, which I and others have elsewhere been developing and defending.[1] This book is not primarily about explaining and advocating personalism, and I do not want my argument in what follows to distract from my main point above, so I am putting this section into an appendix. Still, the uncovering and critiquing of sociology's sacred project that this book is about can benefit by taking a brief note of a genuine alternative to the dominant sacred project that is more adequate for the sociological project of describing, understanding, and explaining human social life. Readers interested in further exploring this personalist alternative will need to study other works to adequately grasp its approach and promise. I cannot do more here than very briefly sketch a handful of its central features, to make the basic point that American sociology's spiritual project is not the only potentially compelling option on offer.

Personalism is a broad philosophical school of thought that developed most clearly as explicit intellectual movements in two different contexts: in continental Europe in the early twentieth century and in Boston, Massachusetts, in the

---

1. For my own work, see Smith, 2010, 2015, 2003.

late nineteenth and early- to mid-twentieth centuries. The school of personalism that I am developing and promote more closely follows the continental European tradition. This European personalist movement, which developed particularly, though not exclusively, among French intellectuals, was unfortunately crushed by the rise of the Nazis in the 1930s and 40s (the Boston personalist movement, not subject to the same threats, evolved more freely into a fifth generation of theorists). The intellectual roots of personalism in both Europe and America draw its life, in various and sometimes indirect ways, from an array of famous and less famous thinkers, about which I have written elsewhere.

The rise of personalism must be properly understood in its philosophical, social, and political context. European personalism offered an alternative to the liberal individualism that had transformed Europe during the eighteenth and nineteenth centuries, by emphasizing the person over the individual and community solidarity over atomization. Indeed, personalism insists on speaking of people as "persons" instead of "individuals," because the former involves natural social ties and obligations while the latter suggests atomistic autonomy. Personalism also arose in part as a response to the intellectual movements of materialism, determinism, and positivism that had so influenced the nineteenth century variously through Marx, Comte, Darwin, Helvétius, and others. European personalism came to fullest fruition in a particularly turbulent socioeconomic and political context of Europe of the 1920s, 30s, and 40s, which shaped the character of its expression. The personalism of this era attempted to raise an intellectual bulwark against both collectivist communism and national socialism, the tides of which were sweeping across Europe, by emphasizing the centrality of the person over the state and economy, and human freedom over totalitarianism. Nazism, however, soon overran that bulwark and repressed and scattered the personalist movement. Many personalist leaders suffered years of suppression by the Nazis and the Vichy regime in France, censorship, loss of jobs, imprisonment, hunger strikes, exile, and sometimes death at early ages. Nazism thus effectively broke up the European personalist movement. (As for Boston personalism, its influence in U.S. philosophy during the twentieth century has for various reasons been limited.) Yet I believe the personalism of the early twentieth century—particularly the realist personalism of Europe—bequeaths to us an intellectual and moral legacy, despite certain ambiguities and problems, that is well worth our retrieving, amending, and developing today.

The crucial point in all such matters, according to personalism, will be any theory or project's view of what human beings are. The view assumed by sociology's sacred project is that human beings are autonomous, self-directing, individual agents living to assert their wills and satisfy their desired pleasures. The sacred project of sociology is simply to help people enjoy being fully what they are. Personalism has the same kind of purpose, but a very different understanding of what human beings are. According to personalism, humans are not individuals but *persons*. And what is a person? Persons in their most developed form are *conscious, reflexive, embodied, self-transcending centers of subjective experience, durable identity, moral commitment, and social communication who—as the efficient cause of their own responsible actions and interactions—exercise complex capacities for agency and inter-subjectivity in order to sustain their own incommunicable selves in loving relationships with other personal selves and with the non-personal world*. That, rightly understood, is a very different understanding of human beings than the view assumed by sociology's sacred project—which carries major consequences for sociology and the world beyond. I explain what all this means elsewhere in depth, and will not repeat it here.[2] For present purposes, suffice it to draw some specific contrasts between sociology's sacred mission and the theory of personalism.

Unlike sociology's sacred mission, personalism is not a fundamentally modern project—its roots are firmly sunk, in fact, in the ancients, particularly in Aristotle. Unlike sociology's sacred project's placing of individual autonomy on the highest pedestal, personalism instead emphasizes human *development, activity*, and *self-realization* that are proper to its natural condition. This underscores another contrast, namely that sociology's sacred project seeks to overcome and transcend the confining constraints of nature, whereas personalism acknowledges humanity's belonging to a *natural* world and is content to work with that fact, including all of its limitations and determinations. Sociology's sacred project believes that humans have no given end or purpose specified by the nature of reality, that people should therefore be free to be and do whatever they individually desire and choose. Personalism, by contrast, believes in a natural human *telos*, a properly good human end toward which people ought to aspire and live. Life is a *quest* to pursue, not a series of constraints from which to be emancipated. The sacred project of American sociology is built on the ontological presupposition of individualism, whereas personalism does not even believe that "the individual" exists—instead what exist are human *persons*, which are quite a different animal. Such an outlook makes considerably better sense of the social world that sociology shows we actually construct and inhabit than does ontological individualism in the homo-duplex tradition.

Sociology's sacred project is committed to the belief that the human will, people's desires, are the ultimate drive in life, whereas personalism understands the *interest* in realizing natural *goods* to be our basic life motivation. The spiritual project of sociology scoffs at the idea of an objectively real moral good—at anything remotely like a natural moral law—claims about which it suspects to be mere oppressive manipulations of the powerful, to be thrown off in moral liberation. Personalism knows that humans are not lost in a world of moral vacuity and relativism, one that cannot reliably guide and govern human desires, but rather

2. Smith, 2010, 2015, 2003.

live in a reality involving natural goods and bads, truths and falsehoods, justices and injustices. And that gives personalism's mission a moral integrity that is missing in sociology's sacred mission, since, in the absence of natural moral goods, any moral commitments that people might make are ultimately arbitrary and so self-undermining.[3] American sociology's sacred project nonetheless insists on the "moral" affirmation of everyone's choices and lifestyle by everyone else in his or her society, an insistence that is mindless and impossible. Personalism distinguishes between those matters about which all humans must be affirmed—or, better, *respected, loved,* and treated with *justice*—and those that instead require their being *challenged,* debated, and sometimes even refused, precisely because they are loved. Sociology's sacred project understands equality to be about the contractually agreed upon right of each individual to demand from others his or her share of human necessities and enjoyments. Personalism grounds equality more fundamentally in a natural human *dignity* that compels everyone to treat everyone else with the proper respect, love, and justice that is proper to his or her personhood.

The current sacred project of American sociology does not quite know what to do with children and other persons who are dependent, vulnerable, and unable to direct their own lives. Personalism, by contrast, draws no sharp lines between children and adults, but in fact sees children as archetypical human beings by virtue of their making clear the real *dependence, need for nurture,* and challenge of growth and *formation* that characterize all humans at every stage of life. Sociology's sacred project is suspicious of social institutions and structures as almost innately oppressive, exploitative, and constraining. Personalism recognizes the powerful capacity and frequent tendency of social institutions and structures to be those things, but more deeply understands them as good and necessary *conditions for human flourishing*—indeed, when constructed and lived well, as *constitutive expressions of human thriving.* Furthermore, American sociology's spiritual project is framed philosophically by a bizarre amalgam of liberalism, positivism, Marxism, empiricism, constructionism, progressivism, hermeneutics, pragmatism, postmodernism, and feminism. Personalism, by contrast, is grounded in the coherent philosophy of neo-Aristotelian critical realism—which refines and integrates the best in sociology's odd philosophical jumble but leaves out the dross. Personalism knows how to hold together ontological realism, epistemological perspectivalism, and judgmental rationality in a way that we can rationally but with humility affirm together the existence of an independent, structured

3. For helpful analyses of the naturalistic approach to morality that personalism embraces and the differences between that and the approach to morality reflected in "public sociology," see Phil Gorski, 2013, "Beyond the Fact/Value Distinction: Ethical Naturalism and the Social Sciences," *Society,* September/October, 50(5), pp. 543–553; Christian Smith, 2013, "Comparing Ethical Naturalism and 'Public Sociology,'" *Society,* September/October, 50(5), pp. 598–601.

reality beyond our minds, while accepting that all human knowledge is culturally and historically situated and conceptually meditated, and still maintaining our human ability to often judge between claims that are right and wrong, truthful and false. American sociology and its sacred project would sometimes like to be able to do something like that, and yet sometimes also wants to flirt in confusion with antirealism and epistemological and cognitive relativism. But toward whichever of these it is attracted, most of American sociology lacks the philosophical framework to do any of this reasonably and coherently.[4]

Sociologists little realize it, but there have been more personalists around than they may suspect. Take Martin Luther King, Jr., for instance. American sociology would like to claim King for its own, since he was a sociology major, an admirable activist and world transformer, and can appear at first glance to be an exemplar of its sacred project. But in fact, King did not support what is the sacred project of sociology today. He was actually a committed personalist, a philosophy he learned from the Boston personalists when studying at Boston University, and was explicit about that.[5] This explains so many of his distinctive commitments and practices—love of enemies, forgiveness of wrongs, nonviolence, reconciliation with adversaries, self-sacrifice, vision for the common good, deep religious convictions, the quest for the beloved community—that are largely absent from American sociology and many of the movements it champions today. Martin Luther King, Jr. would not stand with the dominant project of American sociologists now, however much sociologists would like to own him. He did stand and would stand with the personalist project. Other important personalists that American sociologists may know—and if they do not, they should, if they could possibly do so with an open mind—are Michael Polanyi, Martin Buber, Paul Ricoeur, Emmanuel Levinas, Jacques Maritain, Karol Wojtyla, Dorothy Day, and many others whose thinking and lives are well worth taking seriously, even if we may not fully embrace everything they said and did.

Having sketched these contrasts, the truth of the matter is that personalism and the sacred project of sociology share a number of specific interests and commitments, although usually for different reasons. On some points, the two

4. Sociologists trying to do sociology without the proper kind of grounding in philosophy is like biologists trying to do biology without adequately understanding chemistry, or chemists doing chemistry without a solid understanding of mathematics—it can certainly be done within limits, but it is often misled and stymied, and always curbed in its potential by its background limitations.
5. Martin Luther King, Jr., 1958, "Pilgrimage to Nonviolence," *Fellowship*, Papers 4: 473–481, September 1; revised version later reprinted in a collected volume edited by Fey (*How My Mind Has Changed* [Cleveland: Meridian Books, 1961], pp. 105–115); see Lewis Baldwin and Walter Mueller, 2006, *God and Human Dignity: The Personalism, Theology, and Ethics of Martin Luther King, Jr.*, Notre Dame: University of Notre Dame Press.

are definitely at odds, but on other points, they are not. Sociologists and other sympathetic people who learn personalism will come to see that some of their moral and political commitments are on the right track, but for reasons quite different from those offered by sociology's sacred project. Personalism helps us to understand that those interests and commitments make even better sense when reframed in a personalist understanding. And personalism helps us to see that, when viewed in light of this more coherent and realistic approach, other parts of sociology's spiritual project need to be modified. Once we correct our understanding of what human beings really are—of philosophical anthropology—that has consequences for how we think about the rest of life, society, and the world. Personalism provides the best, most promising way to do that well. At the very least, it shows that sociology's particular sacred project is not the only game in town.

INDEX

INDEX

Macionis, John, 68, 69
Mainline Protestants, 23
Maritain, Jacques, 203
Marks, Loren, 102
Marriage, 55, 58
"marriage premium", 56
Martin, John Levi, 142
Marx, Karl, 74–76, 116, 200
Marxism, x, 9, 11, 20, 25, 64, 126, 128, 202
Massey, Doug, 160
McGill University, 136
Meditation, 66
Megachurches, 43
Melanesian cultures, 84
Mental health, 64
Merton, Robert K., 75, 144
Methodological individualists, 6
Middle Ages, Medieval, 19, 73, 84
"middle-range theory", 141, 144
Militant Islamism, 151
Military draft, 127
Mill, John Stuart, 8
Mills, C. Wright, 119, 126, 144
"Minutemen", 59
Misrecognition, 134, 183
Modernity, 82, 119, 120, 121, 131
Molotch, Harvey, 27
Moral affirmation, 7, 13, 14, 16, 17, 19, 202
Mormon (LDS), 23, 163
Moses, 125
Muller, Jerry, 3
Multiculturalism, 72
Muslim women, 45
Myth of "monolithic evangelism", 45

"narcissism of small differences", 141
National Council on Family Relations, 104
National Longitudinal Lesbian Family Study, 107
National Science Foundation, 98, 108
Naturalism, ix
Natural environment, 14
Natural goods, 201, 202
Nazis, 200

New Athiest, 36
New digital media, 49
New Family Structures Study (NFSS), 102–103
New York, 126
New York Hilton, 117
Nicaragua, 151
Nihilism, 19
Nisbet, Robert, 131
Nominalism, 19
Nonviolence, 203
North Carolina, 36

Obama, President Barack, 112
"old-boy" networks, 83
Olympics, 76
Ontological realism, 202

Paradigms, 146
Parsons, Talcott, 75, 126, 127, 128
Patriarchy, 13, 82
"Pax Wisconsana", 142
Peer-review system, 109, 155–172, 182
Pentecostalism, 151
Perfectibility of mankind, 124
Personalism, 204
"the personal is political", 139
Perspectivalists, 166
Peterson, Richard, 97–98, 101
Philosophers, 72, 76
Philosophy, 70, 88, 135, 143, 144, 203
Philosophical anthropology, 7, 14, 16, 204
"plausible deniability", 7
Pluralism, 148
Poland, 40
Polanyi, Michael, 165, 203
"political insensitivity", 111
Polyamorous marriage, 81
Pope Gregory, 74
Populist, 26
Positivism, 8, 23, 77–78, 126, 202
Postmodernism, 10–11, 25, 92, 202
Poststructuralism, 10–11, 25
Poverty, 13, 78, 117, 126, 189
Pragmatism, 9, 11, 25, 202

Premarital sex, 84
Prison violence, 80
Progress, 124, 146
Progressive social reform, 9, 13, 202
Progressive fundamentalism, 145
"project", 3
Prostitution, 40, 84
Protestant, 18, 126
Provosts, 179, 180
Psychology as religion, 4
"public sociology", 64, 202

Queer theory, 84

Race, class, and gender, 22, 85
Racism, 13, 70, 80
Radcliffe College, 98
Radical, 12, 79
Rationalistic, ix
Rational-choice, 25
Rauschenbusch, Walter, 9
Realism, 26
Redding, Richard, 107
"red-state" middle Americans, 27
Reed, Ralph, 152
Reformist, 11, 20, 25
"regeneration", 73
Regnerus, Mark, 101–114, 157–172, 194
Relativism, 19
Religion, 13, 16, 27, 72, 84, 123, 124, 151,
    152, 164, 165, 203
"Religion of Humanity", 8
Religious "fundamentalists", 163
Religious proselytizing, 44, 134
Religious right, 43, 45, 145, 151
Religious Studies, 91
Religious wars, 120
Reproductive choice, 70
Revolutions, 65
Ricoeur, Paul, 203
Right-wing, 27, 155
Risman, Barbara, 35
Roberts, Robin, of ABC News, 112
Robertson, Pat, 152
de Robespierre, Maximilien, 155
Robinson, Jackie, 77

Rock-and-roll, 127
Roman Catholic Vatican Curia, 122
Roof, Wade Clark, 151
Rosenberg, Harold, 146
Rosenfeld, Michael, 108
Ross, Edward, 123, 124
Rowling, J.K., 113
The Roy Scrivner fund of the American
    Psychological Association, 106
Rytina, Steve, 136

Sacred, 1, 2, 5, 6
Sacred gnosis, 116
Salvation, 125
Same-sex relationships, 103, 111
Same-sex marriages, 40, 69, 81
San Francisco, 61
Sanger, Margaret, 9
Schaefer, Richard, 68
Schumm, Walter, 111
Schwalbe, Michael, 36–37
"the scientific method", 5, 122
science, 116, 165, 166
"scientific" minority of sociologists, 161
Scientism, 166
Secular, ix, x, 3, 13, 120, 122
Secular salvation gospel, 20
Secularization theory, 150, 151
Segregation, 65
Sex education, 36
Sexist male pigs, 128
Sexual behaviors, 57
Sexual orientation, 16, 82, 84, 85
Sexual revolution, 10, 11, 20, 25, 84,
    85, 89
Shia Muslims, 25
Slate, 102, 112
Small, Albion, 122, 123
Smith, Adam, 8
Social breakdown, 49
Social capital, 48, 49
Social class, 50, 64, 70, 75, 81, 82, 96
Social control, 122
Social constructionism, 11, 25, 77, 82, 128,
    153, 154, 173, 195–196, 202
Social demographers, 89, 92

Social Forces, 29
Social Gospel, ix, 9, 123
Social Isolation, 48, 49
Social laws, 123
Social movements, 7, 12, 18, 124, 127, 153
Social networks, 48, 53
Social Science Research, 102, 107, 109, 158, 161
Social Science Research Council, 97
"sociography", 184–185
"Sociological imagination", 13
Sociological Research Association, 137
Sociologists as scientific experts, 40
Sociology as the "Queen of Sciences", 8
Sociology as a "multiple paradigm science", 147
Sociology Internet blogs, 166
Sociology the "science-of-social-life", 5, 26, 34, 47, 134, 135
Sociology of religion, x
Sociological orthodoxy, 7
Solidarność, 151
The (American) South, 44, 92
Southern, 87
South African apartheid, 151
"specialization-induced intellectual poverty", 143
Spencer, Herbert, 75
Spiritual, x, 2, 3, 5
Spiritual but not religious, 3
Stacy, Judith, 85
Stalin, Joseph, 155
State programs and regulations, 12
Status-oriented nature of sociology, 136
Steinmetz, George, 126
Stereotypes, 80, 82
Structural-functionalism, 74–76, 79, 125, 126
Stryker, Sheldon, 76
Student free speech movement, 127, 129
Suffering, 67, 189
Sufism, 25
Sunni Muslims, 25
Sweden, 35, 36
Symbolic-interactionism, 74–76, 79

The Tea Party, 96
Tenure and promotion, 94, 182
Textbooks, 68–86, 100, 123
Thatcher, Margaret, 181
Therapeutic culture, 9, 11, 20, 25
Third-wave feminism, 10
Thomism, 66
Thornton, Arland, 99
Time, 81
Totalitarianism, 24, 200
Tocqueville, Alexis de, 73
Transsexuals, 84
Trojan condoms, 107
"true believers", 24, 161

Unemployment, 70
United Methodist Church, 163
Unionization, 52, 58
Unitarian Universalist, 25, 91
University of Central Florida, 109–110
University of Chicago, 89
University of North Carolina-Chapel Hill, 87, 91
University of Texas at Austin, 90, 101, 107, 113
University of Virginia, 174
U.S. Congress, 100
U.S. Labor Market, 51
U.S./Mexican border, 59
U.S. Supreme Court, 100, 109

Value-free, 78, 125
Versailles, 196
Vichy regime, 200
Vietnam war, 127
Vincent, George, 122, 123
Virtues, 66, 165
Virtuous conflict, 140
Voltaire, 8
Voyeurism, 45

Wald, Lillian, 9
Ward, Lester, 122, 123, 124
Weber, Max, x, 116, 120
Weberian sociology, 147
Weitzman, Lenore, 97–101